The Writing Workshop

A World of Difference

The Writing Workshop

A World of Difference

A GUIDE FOR STAFF DEVELOPMENT

Lucy McCormick Calkins
Shelley Harwayne

Teachers College Writing Project
Teachers College
Columbia University

HEINEMANN, Portsmouth, NH

Heinemann
A division of Reed Elsevier Inc.
361 Hanover Street Portsmouth, NH 03801-3912
Offices and agents throughout the world

10   9   8   7   6

Cover photo by Peter Michaels.
Designed by Wladislaw Finne.
Printed in the United States of America.
0-435-08450-X

Contents

1 Introduction   1

2 Staff Development in Writing   5

  A Broad View of Staff Development   6
  Planning a Workshop for Teachers: Arrangements   8
  Planning a Workshop for Teachers: Content   9
  The First Five Minutes   11
  General Suggestions for Staff Development   12
  Predictable Problems   13
  Predictable Benefit   15
  Selected Readings   15

3 First Viewing   17

  Overview of the Tape   17
  When Only One Viewing Can Be Arranged   18
  Selected Readings   19

4 Reasons to Write   21

  Investment in Writing   22
    Probes   23
      Choosing Topics That Matter   23
      Rethinking the Reasons and the Routines for Share
        Meetings   24

Materials That Encourage Purposeful Writing   25
Responses That Encourage Purposeful Writing   25

Activities   26

Time Lines of Growth in Writing   26
Brainstorming Ways to Increase Student Investment in
   Writing   26
Highlight the Need for Purposeful Writing   27

Strategies for Finding Topics   27

Probes   29

Major Revisions Become Rehearsal   29
Disposable Writing   29
Beyond Topic Choice   29
When Writers Can't Find Topics   30
Topics with Potential   30

Activities   30

Anticipate and Address Concerns over Topic Choice   30
Bring Home the Issues of Topic Choice   31
Research the Relationship Between Topic Choice and Writing
   Development   31

Selected Readings   32

5   *The Structure of a Writing Workshop*   33

Probes   36

Planning for a Writing Workshop   36
There's No One Way to Teach Writing   37
The Predictable Structure and the Rules That Undergird
   the Writing Workshop   38
Convey Respect for Tools and Materials   38
Select Tools with Care   38
The Reading Table   39

Activities   39

Reflect on the Hubbub of the Writing Workshop   39
Draw a Floor Plan   40
Classrooms That Convey a Respect for Craftsmanship   40
Classrooms Reflect Changing Priorities   40

Selected Readings   40

6   Early Writing   43

  Probes   47

    Elicit a Story From a Drawing   47
    Encourage Children to Move from Drawing to Writing   47
    Use the Drawing for Context Clues   48
    Teach Spelling Strategies   48
    The Issue of Spelling Errors   48

  Activities   48

    Refer to Recommended Readings   48
    Bring Children into the Staff Development Sessions   49
    Simulate the Classroom   49
    Case-Study Research as the Centerpiece in Staff
      Development   50
    An Early Childhood Videotape   50
    Study and Observe Children's Spelling Strategies   50

  Selected Readings   51

7   Conferring: The Heart of the Writing Workshop   53

  Probes   56

    Conferring Changes Once the Workshop Is Well
      Established   56
    Myths of Conferring   56
    More Myths of Conferring   56
    New Ideas on Teaching Writing Affect Teacher-Student
      Conferences   57
    Critiquing the Videotaped Conferences   57
    Each Conference Occurs Within a Context   58
    Revision of Teaching   58
    The Importance of Audience   59

  Activities   59

    Categorize Teacher-Student Conferences   59
    Role-Plays That Illustrate the Guidelines for Effective
      Conferences   59
    Learning to Shorten Conferences   60
    Analyze the Videotaped Conferences   61
    Beyond Content Conferences   61

Personal Style and Conferring   62
Cross-References to Other Conferring Activities   62

Selected Readings   62

8   Literature: The Most Crucial Resource in a Writing Workshop   63

Stories of Authors' Lives   63

Probes   64

Take Cues from the Writer   64
Select One Thing to Teach   65
Leave Room for the Writer   65

Activities   65

Weave Author Anecdotes into Conferences   65
Develop a File of Author Anecdotes   66
Use Author Anecdotes to Introduce New Tools and Rituals   66

Using Literature as a Resource for Learning About Good
Writing   67

Probes   68

Students Read and Write Within the Same Genre   68
Maintain a Broad View of Literature   68

Activities   69

Conferring with a Book Under One's Arm   69
More Ways to Weave Literature into Conferences   70
Common Problems in Mini-Lessons   70
Dramatize the Need to Take Cues from Students   70

Selected Readings   71

9   Transcript of the Video "The Writing Workshop: A World of Difference"   73

10   Workshop Materials   87

Workshop Materials A: Viewers' Sheet   89
Workshop Materials B: Two-Column Log   94

Workshop Materials C: Dilemmas Surrounding Topic Choice 95

Workshop Materials D: Discussion of Dilemmas Surrounding Topic Choice 97

Workshop Materials E: Dwayne's Writing Folder 99

Workshop Materials F: The Spelling Strategies of Our Young Writers 121

Workshop Materials G: Reflections on the Spelling Strategies of Our Young Writers 125

Workshop Materials H: General Instructions for Creating a Character for a Role-Play 127

Workshop Materials I: Donald Murray's Guidelines for Conferring 130

Workshop Materials J: Using Stories from Authors' Lives as Resources in Conferences 132

Workshop Materials K: Stories from Authors' Lives 134

Workshop Materials L: Building Files of Author Stories 138

Workshop Materials M: Authors' Anecdotes That Could Inspire New Classroom Rituals, Tools, or Traditions 140

Workshop Materials N: Discussion of Authors' Anecdotes That Could Inspire New Classroom Rituals, Tools, or Traditions 142

Workshop Materials O: Situations That Can Lead to Mini-Lessons Using Literature 143

Workshop Materials P: Discussion of Situations That Can Lead to Mini-Lessons Using Literature 145

Bibliography 147

1

Introduction

These are exciting times in the teaching of writing. For the first time, we have major studies on how students develop as writers. Findings from these studies have begun to echo each other and to provide new insights on the teaching of writing. A new paradigm has emerged, and as it has been implemented, tested, refined, and enriched, it has led to new areas of investigation: reading-writing connections, purposeful writing, writing in a range of genres. None of these ideas matter, however, unless they reach classrooms.

Thankfully, the new knowledge base on teaching writing has been accompanied by a growing interest in staff development. Through university courses, in-service workshops, summer institutes, and schoolwide release days, teachers are learning about the teaching of writing. For those of us who lead these courses of study, the challenge is not only to show teachers that new ideas can be translated into practice, but also to issue what Janet Emig calls a generous invitation, encouraging teachers to become insiders in the field of writing—developing, implementing, and refining ideas of their own. This is crucially important, because it is in classrooms that ideas must take root and grow. The field of teaching writing belongs in the hands of teachers.

It is appropriate, therefore, that most staff development in writing begins first with teachers meeting in response groups, developing, sharing, and rethinking drafts of their own writing. In these interactive forums, teachers make discoveries for themselves and teach each other what they know. They come from these sessions saying, "I feel so much better about my own writing; I have a repertoire of strategies now to draw upon and an image of what it means to write well."

Then, in the second component of staff development, teachers attend sessions on methods of working with young writers. They often come from these sessions with spiral notebooks filled with adages, definitions, and lists of suggestions. "I'm so overwhelmed," they say. "I feel so insecure about the prospect of teaching writing."

Ideally, teachers should be sharing the "rough drafts" of their classrooms. Ideally, they should be listening not only to each other's texts but also to each other's teaching. In both crafts, writing and teaching writing, teachers need the grounding and confidence necessary to be pioneers, asking questions and inventing ideas. This is most apt to happen if staff development in writing involves teachers in both active and interactive ways. We created this videotape in part because visiting each other's classrooms is not always possible. Because this video is comprised of classroom episodes and scenes, and because most of the voices on it are those of teachers and children, the tape serves almost as a visit to effective writing classrooms.

The wonderful thing about visiting our colleagues' classrooms is that the visits provide natural opportunities for good, professional talk. The video, of course, is meant not as a replacement for this sort of interaction but as the impetus for it. Just as rough drafts of writing are meant to be shared, so too, these scenes and episodes are meant to be discussed.

This guide has been written with two goals in mind. We want to help staff development leaders use the videotape easily and well, and we want to help with the crucially important task of teaching teachers. Readers will quickly notice that instead of providing ready-made lesson plans for staff development sessions, the guide provides a storehouse of staff development ideas and insights on teaching writing. Chapters 2 and 3 address general issues, and chapters 4 through 8 address thematic topics that might each be the focus of one or more staff development sessions. These chapters are sequenced according to the logic we might use in a course on teaching writing. For example, the first thematic chapter, "Reasons to Write," addresses issues such as motivation, launching the writing workshop, the importance of selecting good topics, and ways to help youngsters write with purpose and consequence. This provides a base for later topics, such as reading-writing connections and conferring.

This does not mean, however, that the first chapters of the book pertain only to uninitiated teachers of writing and that the later sections are more pertinent for experienced writing process teachers. Instead, within each chapter our newest thoughts, questions, and perspectives have been woven into familiar and essential ideas on teaching writing. Teachers and children who have spent years working in writing process classrooms will probably find, for example, that within the early chapters there are many new ideas on purposeful writing, ways to provide diverse audiences for student writers, and methods for helping students flesh out their writing through rehearsal and research.

Although this guide does discuss ways to introduce the writing process to teachers who are new to these ideas, it assumes that those who use it are familiar with writing process ideas in general and with Calkins's book, *The Art of Teaching Writing*, in particular. Readers will find that the book is referred to often, and they will probably want each participant in their staff development workshop to have his or her own copy of it.

Although the guide is meant more as a resource to be used than as a book to be read, workshop leaders will want to study the entire guide before beginning staff development sessions. We especially recommend that you read it with the needs and talents of your teachers in mind. You may decide to ask some workshop participants to lead some of the sessions, in which case it may help to give them copies of this guide. You may decide to provide participants with a packet of readings or to give each one a single, wonderful piece of children's literature to use throughout the course. Or you may ask each participant to do a case study of his or her students throughout the duration of the course. Long-range plans such as these can bind your course of study into a cohesive whole.

In reading through the guide, you will see that the chapters 4 through 8 share a common structure: they each begin with an overview of the topic. Then the sections of the videotape that pertain to that specific topic are listed and summarized and counter numbers are given to indicate the location of each episode within the videotape. These counter numbers allow you to replay selected sections for the teachers in your workshop or as part of your preparation for the session. (Because of variations in individual types of VCRs, the counter numbers provided in this guide may not be accurate for all videocassette players.) Each chapter also has a section entitled "Probes," which contains insights, questions, and concerns that are important to us. As a workshop leader, you may want to raise some of these issues in your discussions with participating teachers. The probes are not organized in any significant fashion because we do not intend that they provide a course of study so much as a storehouse of ideas and insights. Following the probes, each chapter contains a collection of workshop activities. Again, you should view these as resources that can be condensed, adapted, combined, and altered. Activities listed in one chapter will often spark ideas for activities that could have been listed under other chapter headings. Sometimes one activity will lead into another, while at other times an activity stands best on its own. In each chapter, some of the activities and probes involve staff development materials. Wherever it seemed appropriate to do so, we have developed prototype materials. They are contained in the final section of the book, "Workshop Materials."

Each chapter ends with a brief reading list. The articles and books cited have been chosen from a huge number of available references, and they are ones we highly recommend.

Dig in, then. Make yourself at home. Cut the guide into pieces and restructure it according to the logic of your own teaching. Discard some of our probes and add your own. Above all, put aside this guide and listen to your students. Maimonides was wise when he said, "I have learned much from my teachers, more from my friends, and most from my students."

2

Staff Development in Writing

Recently an article came out in the *New York Times* about our staff development work in New York City schools. The article, "Young Authors in the South Bronx," told about children who draft and revise their own stories and poems, publishing them in laminated books. Shortly after the article was printed, the Writing Project received a phone call from a principal in another borough. "We're interested in bringing writing process to our schools," he said, and so Lucy Calkins began explaining how people from the Teachers College Writing Project work with a cadre of interested teachers, leading demonstration lessons, coaching and supporting them in their classrooms, and meeting with them in after-school workshops. "No, no, you've got me wrong," the principal interrupted. "What we're interested in is the laminating machine. Where did you get it?" After Lucy read off the supply catalog number, the man hung up, thankful he could now buy a machine that would bring writing process to his district.

We laugh, but he is not the only one wanting to buy writing process. At state and national conferences, the exhibition halls are filled with writing kits and textbooks. We now have prewriting skill sheets and revision checklists. Recently a colleague of ours received a letter saying, "I hear you are doing interesting things in staff development. Would you please send them in the enclosed self-addressed envelope."

The most important thing we could put in that envelope was a list of names and phone numbers. "These people are experts on teaching writing," we wrote. "It's people who can make everything else possible."

Effective staff development is not dependent upon kits, skill sheets, videotapes, or guidebooks, but upon people. When districts phone for advice as they plan staff development, we always suggest that an early priority must be to help certain teachers become experts.

But even experts in teaching writing need assistance and support in order to lead staff development workshops. The challenge of teaching teachers is different from the challenge of teaching children. Ideally, leaders of staff development should be able to attend courses and join support groups that focus on the issue of staff development. Because this is not always possible, we have tried to compile some of our suggestions into this chapter.

A Broad View of Staff Development

By the time teachers file into a room, ready for the start of a course of study, crucial decisions have already been made. Because these decisions will determine the effectiveness of staff development, those of us who are asked to lead these sessions cannot sit by and let others make these broad-ranging decisions for us.

Even if we are invited to lead a workshop on a very specific topic, we think it is important to ask if the specifics are negotiable and to become involved in shaping the design of the staff development session. It is also important to be willing to say no rather than to lead a staff development session that is doomed from the start.

Most of us believe that it is preferable to work with teachers over a long period of time, to work only with teachers who have chosen to participate, to provide time for teachers to write together, to have classroom-based follow-up, and so forth. But the truth is that it is possible to provide wise staff development within all sorts of less-than-ideal conditions provided we tailor our goals and methods to fit the needs of participating teachers and the constraints of the situation. There *are* wise ways to work with an angry group of teachers facing the mandated adoption of a new approach toward teaching writing, but the goal of such a workshop might well be to have administrators and teachers talking to, arguing with, and listening to each other about the issues that surround the notion of mandated curriculum development. It is not entirely foolish to have a two-hour session that provides an overview of ideas on teaching writing process, but clearly, such a session should be an invitation for teachers to learn more about the field of teaching writing. Such a session should emphasize ways to learn more rather than ways to immediately change one's classroom practices.

The important thing is to have a match between methods and goals and to be clear about what is and is not possible within the constraints of the situation.

Oftentimes it is easy for workshop leaders to influence the design of staff development. If this is so, they may want to consider these suggestions:

- Usually it is easier to work with a group of teachers who share a specific interest and background than with a very eclectic group. In the Teachers College Writing Project, when we divide teachers of writing into grade-level sections, we try to have a K–1 or K–2 section, and a 2–6 or 3–6 section, and one for secondary-level teachers. We do not divide into grade-level groups according to the very common K–3 and 4–8 divisions.
- We find it harder to provide a broad overview of the writing process than to lead workshops on narrower topics. Many specific topics, however, are only appropriate if attending teachers have background knowledge on writing process. For example, it probably does not make sense to lead a workshop on revision, authors as mentors, or peer response groups unless participants have an overall image of an effective writing workshop. There are some topics, however, that can stand on their own. These include the use of learning logs across the curriculum, the need to develop a schoolwide or classroom policy on editing, and the ways writing can be used as a tool for responding to literature.
- It is helpful to establish a long-term schedule that allows participating teachers to anticipate and plan for all the workshops that will occur over the course of the year.
- Myriad problems arise sometimes from the well-intentioned decision to target staff development toward a particular grade level. For example, a district that plans to train K–1 teachers first and then "work up the grades" should realize that teachers in the upper elementary and middle school grades rarely want to inherit a program that began at the kindergarten level. On the other hand, it is a shame to exclude primary teachers from staff development because often these are the teachers who will have the easiest time turning classrooms into writing workshops. Then, too, if any one grade level is targeted, often this means that some of those teachers must be prodded to participate. We find that the best plan, then, is simply to encourage interested teachers to participate and hope that those teachers represent a wide range of grade levels.
- In kindergarten classrooms, young children plant kidney beans in milk cartons in order to learn the slowness of growth. Educators who plan for and lead staff development would be wise to do the same. Anything worth learning takes time, lots and lots of time. We advise districts against the idea that one group of teachers will be trained one year, and that the training will then move to a whole new group. If two or three

groups of teachers need to be trained, we suggest that districts plan to spend several years working with one group. While continuing to work with the first group, workshop leaders can also find ways to work with the second group.

Planning a Workshop for Teachers: Arrangements

When we first led workshops for teachers, we were so concerned over whether we would have anything to say that we spent our planning time thinking about the words to come out of our mouths. We filled index cards and memorized informal-sounding speeches. How easy it is to forget that in teaching adults, as in teaching children, the arrangements we establish are more important than the words out of our mouths.

A classroom teacher naturally begins planning the year by asking big questions. What will we study and in what sequence? Will there be a textbook? What will the schedule look like? How much time can we devote to a subject? Will there be reading groups, and what will distinguish one group from another? What kinds of materials will I need, and what will my students need? What work can I expect outside of class? How will the room be arranged?

We need to ask these same questions when planning staff development—and of course, the answers depend on our long-range goals. When Lucy Calkins worked in the Guilderland school system five years ago, she and the associate superintendent designed her work to establish ongoing structures that would encourage teachers in each building to learn alongside each other, even when Calkins was not there. Calkins came to the district six times, and her visits were scheduled for the first Tuesday of the month. During each visit, she worked in two school buildings, and in each instance, roving substitute teachers freed several teachers at a time so that from 9:00 A.M. to 10:00 A.M., for example, three third-grade teachers worked with Calkins in a third-grade classroom, meeting afterwards to talk. During their meeting with Calkins, the third-grade teachers would identify shared concerns and devise ways to explore these concerns over the course of the month. The substitute teachers returned to these buildings every Tuesday to allow teachers to continue observing in each other's classrooms.

On each of her visits, Calkins ended the day with an after-school workshop for forty teachers. The teachers sat at five round tables, and each table was led by a teacher-facilitator who then met with Calkins for a planning supper at the end of the day. These facilitators also led after-school and lunchtime meetings in their buildings throughout the month.

There is nothing magical about this particular structure, but it is an example of the way staff development arrangements can fit the situation in an individual school district.

Planning a Workshop for Teachers: Content

We need to plan not only the design of staff development but also the content. In the Writing Project, we generally begin not by thinking of activities, anecdotes, or specific tips we can give on a topic, but instead by trying to select and organize the overarching ideas of the workshop. For example, if we are designing a workshop to help teachers make reading-writing connections, we might decide that the central idea could be that young people need to feel they are insiders in the world of writers. This idea could be developed by telling stories about the kinds of connections children can make with authors if the youngsters see themselves as authors. This theme could be developed with answers to the question "How, then, can we make young people feel they are insiders in the world of authors?" At this point, notes for the staff development session might look like this:

- Reading-writing connections that result from insider status.
- Why important? (Stories, examples)
- How to make kids insiders in the world of writers?
  1. Time to do a good job on their writing (rehearse, revise, etc.).
  2. Writing real literature, not school compositions.
  3. Natural forms of publication—not merely bulletin boards.

Before spending time fleshing out a map such as this one, we try to pull back and look at it critically. In this instance, what began as a workshop on reading-writing connections has become an introduction to ideas on teaching writing. For this particular group of teachers, the information isn't new enough. Back at the drawing board, we devise and then reject several other "maps." Finally, we decide that the central point might be that in order to help young people make reading-writing connections, teachers need to make books more accessible and more human, and they need to help children view their writing as more like literature. Now the map of the session looks like this:

Reading
- Books are written by real people: author studies, many books by one author.
- The power of a single, "fully inhabited" book: rereading, becoming at home within a book.

- Ways to structure book-talk.
- Etc.

Writing

- The writing often looks like written-down show and tell. Do the kids even intend to write literature?
- Rethinking how we introduce the idea of writing to kids.
- When kids read their writing aloud, it is not like when they read literature aloud.
  Will storytelling help?
- Small ways we convey respect/disrespect for children's writing:
  —Do we read it aloud only during writing workshop?
  —Is it kept in the school library?

It helps to devise at least a tentative working map of a staff development session many weeks prior to the session because then we have the time to live with the topic, accumulating insights, anecdotes, and specific tips. We usually keep a spiral notebook of related ideas and a file of related articles, anecdotes, quotations, and children's pieces.

We find information that relates to the topic in surprising places. From a recent *National Geographic* we learned that pigs are not dirty but clean, and that doves, far from being peaceful, will eat each other alive. Although we do not lead workshops on doves and pigs, this tidbit of information reminds us of how important it is to question one's assumptions—and certainly this is true for assumptions about reading. Information on pigs and doves, then, is added to the file on reading.

Our research usually involves looking in a special way at children. We sort through many writing folders, conduct class surveys, and interview selected students. We also interview teachers, and we phone colleagues around the country. "Do you know any little jokes on assessment?" we recently asked Nancie Atwell. There was a long pause on the other end of the phone and then Nancie answered, "There are no *little* jokes on assessment." And that comment became the lead-in to a workshop.

When planning the details of a workshop, we work from an excess of information. We usually have enough material for a whole course before we begin to flesh out the workshop plan, and this excess of information helps us to be selective and to have high standards.

Above all, planning a workshop involves selection. The issue is never how to fill the time, but instead, how to use each moment wisely. "Of all that we could do, what is the single most important way we can use this time?" is the guiding question. Only after we have a sense of the entire workshop can we begin to think about how and where in the plans we should insert activities. Decisions about whether to use one activity or another are made only after we have a sense of the whole.

The First Five Minutes

We find it important to remember that a staff development session does not begin when the leader clears his or her throat, signaling for attention. It begins, instead, when the first participant enters the room. These early moments are important ones; they provide a time for learning people's names, for discovering something about the teachers who will comprise the group. One has just returned to teaching after ten years at home raising children. Another attended a similar workshop last month. A third has been reading Elbow's book, *Embracing Contraries*. Still another has tried these ideas and they didn't work for her.

These early moments can also give us an opportunity to raise the low expectations teachers often have of a staff development session. They often enter the room expecting to sit passively and wait with glassy eyes until the workshop is over. If they sit at the back of the room and put a stack of student papers on the desk in front of them, they do this for a reason: they have learned from experience not to have high hopes about staff development.

We begin changing expectations just by greeting participants as they enter. We can also cue teachers to the fact that this workshop will be different if we arrange chairs in circles, bring a tablecloth for the coffee table, and have strawberries, cheese, and real cream for the coffee. These little details are not little at all.

Then, too, what we say to open the workshop matters. "I'm not good at jokes," people have said, not realizing that jokes do not come easily to us either. We may spend a week searching for a joke to use at the start of a speech or workshop. But we are also not convinced that a workshop must begin with jokes. It must begin with energy and with a sense of personal connection. Even if we will eventually speak from notes, we try to begin by putting aside the pages of notes, coming out from behind the podium or table, and simply being there, with colleagues and with ideas that are urgently important to us.

We convey that urgency, that enthusiasm, by starting workshops on time. Our actions say, "We don't want to waste a precious moment." We also convey urgency by giving people an agenda for the session.

Sometimes the first activity in a workshop involves introductions among the participants. Depending on the total length of time participants will spend together and on how well they already know each other, we vary the thoroughness and manner of these introductions. We may do any of these:

1 Ask people to make a name plaque that contains a self-portrait. Then we can begin by referring to insecurities over drawing, and likening them to insecurities over writing.

2 Take an oral survey of the group. "How many of you love to write?" "How many of you teach K–1 students?" etc.

3 Ask people to divide into pairs and interview each other. Then each person introduces his or her partner to the group by telling one (only) detail about the person. Halfway through this we have a "quiz" so as to remind people to listen aggressively and make a real effort to remember each other's names.

4 We sometimes begin by asking people to clear their desks off in preparation for an examination. Then we have passed out a written survey with questions such as "Find someone who has the same favorite author as you do: _____." "Name two people whose questions about teaching writing resemble yours: _____, _____."

5 We might ask people to jot down some thoughts on two or three crucial topics. One might be, "When, in your life, have you felt like an author?" Another might be, "What person has helped your writing the most? What did that person say or do?" Then people share responses (and their names) in small groups.

General Suggestions for Staff Development

In good teaching, like good writing, it is crucially important to find one's own voice. This comes with time, but it helps if you trust your instincts, teach on topics you know and care about, and listen for when your teaching works well. One person may do best when teaching without notes, another when the workshop has been carefully planned. Try as best you can to know your own strengths and play into them.

Then, too, we can learn about teaching teachers by watching others around us and learning from their struggles and their successes. The Writing Project has a library of tape-recorded workshops, and we listen to them not only to learn information, but also to think about the qualities of an effective workshop.

We have noticed, for example, that when we attend workshops and listen to other people's speeches, we appreciate it if we are given some sense of the exoskeleton of that person's talk. If the person says, "There are three crucial elements . . ." then we can organize our notes into general categories and anticipate what will come next in the session. When reading a written text, we can look ahead to see the number of remaining pages, and we have subheadings to convey emphasis. Workshop leaders can find ways to provide their own sort of subheadings.

We have also learned that the building block of a workshop is the specific example, the anecdote. This not only means that we try to find stories and anecdotes that convey our messages, but also that we try to elicit *specifics* from participants in the workshop. Instead of asking, "How should we respond to student writing?" we show a piece of writing and ask, "What would you say if Peter brought you this draft?" Instead of asking, "What helps your writing?" we ask, "What is the single most helpful thing anyone ever said to you about your writing?"

It is important to remember that we teach not only by what we say but also by how we say it. All the talk in the world about the need to give teachers ownership does not undo the message we convey if our thoughts about teaching writing are hooked onto "you shoulds." What a different message we convey if, instead of saying, "You should have two sets of writing folders," we say, "Often teachers find it helpful to store students' writing in folders."

Workshops that are ostensibly about the teaching of writing can also be about broad, crucial topics: listening to students, the need to slow down the school day, the need for us, as teachers, to take time for our own reading and writing. We can't easily lecture on topics such as these, but we say something about these issues, for example, when we talk about specific children, calling them by name rather than speaking of them as if there is such a thing as a generic student. Equally important is the message we convey when we credit our own mentors and refer to the sources of our ideas. Professional learning involves standing on the shoulders of others and joining a community of learners. Similarly, we convey something important when we speak with tentativeness. If someone asks what to do about the child who hates to write, instead of responding with a definitive answer we suggest that the teacher try a few things and watch to see what happens, or we open the question up to the group, asking for their ideas. These responses say, "Join me in thinking about this problem," and "There is no one, right answer." The tone and tentativeness of our response conveys something crucial about the teaching of writing.

Predictable Problems

The leader of a staff development workshop would be wise to anticipate that the slide projector may not work, the printing on a crucial transparency may be too small for people to read, the administrators who attend the workshop may stand at the back of the room talking with each other, and people may interrupt with so many questions that you lose your train of thought and finish only half of what you'd planned. It is helpful to think in advance about ways of responding to predictable problems such as these.

Many of the problems are not unique to working with adults. Every teacher struggles during his or her first few years of teaching with an inability to estimate the time an activity will take. These early struggles haunt us again when we teach within the new context of a staff development course. It may help to plan the workshop anticipating the amount of time each section will take, then marking the quarter and halfway points on your notes so that you can see early on whether you are running behind your scheduled plans and can choose to delete particular sections from the middle of the workshop rather than simply not reaching the end of it. Then, too, many people plan for workshops with an eye towards which sections could be deleted or expanded, depending on which is necessary. Many people end a workshop with a time for questions and answers. Their biggest fear is, "What if no one asks a question?" One way around this is to begin the question-and-answer session by asking each person to jot down three questions and to star the most important one. This ensures that everyone will have a question and therefore that the workshop will not need to end early.

This is not usually the problem, however. More often, workshop leaders find that every activity takes longer than they had planned. "How can I speed up the pace?" they ask. It helps to remember that administrative details tend to take as much time as they are given. If announcements are squeezed into the last few minutes of a workshop, then the discussion of them can be done individually among people who linger after the workshop is over with questions.

It also helps if workshop leaders recognize the effectiveness of two- or three-minute activities. If a workshop leader wants to emphasize that teachers need to be readers as well as writers, the leader could ask each participant to bring his or her favorite book to the workshop, and one by one the participants could stand and share the chosen book. But would it not be almost as effective if the workshop leader simply paused and said, "Would you think for a moment about the very most special book you've ever read," and then said, "Tell your neighbor the title of the book, and try, also, to tell why the book made such an impact on you." Then again, it takes only several minutes for people to brainstorm the ways a learning log can be used in conjunction with a film on the Civil War, or for teachers to recall (and share with one person) the most helpful thing anyone ever said to them about their writing. There are countless other three-minute activities, and most of them are as effective as activities which take much more time.

Then, too, it helps to listen to tape recordings of one's own teaching and to study the passage of time. When did things drag—and why? When did the pace seem hectic? From tape recording and studying one's own workshop, it is easy to see the ways time is wasted. Perhaps tasks such as handing out articles or collecting papers are done in a time-consuming manner. Perhaps there seems to be an assumption that whenever people work in small groups, each group needs to report back.

One of the most common of the problems we encounter are the urgent questions participants ask throughout a workshop. Some workshop leaders thrive on these questions, but others (including ourselves) find that receiving a barrage of questions interrupts our frame of thought and leads to a splintered and hasty discussion of a thousand vaguely related topics. Therefore, when early on in a workshop a participant asks a question, you might say, "That is such an important question, but. . . ." Pausing, you may look at everyone and say, "Can I ask all of you to jot down your questions when you have them, and then we'll stop periodically to deal with them."

Predictable Benefit

Erik Erikson has said, "Human beings are constituted so as to need to teach. Ideas are kept alive by being shared, truths by being professed." Staff development leaders will find that sharing ideas on teaching makes them both more reflective and more dedicated as classroom teachers. They will find that there is a fine line between teaching others how to teach and teaching oneself how to teach.

Selected Readings

Barth, Roland. *Run School Run.* Cambridge, MA: Harvard University Press, 1980.

Lortie, Dan. *Schoolteacher: A Sociological Study.* Chicago: University of Chicago Press, 1977.

Sarason, Seymour. *The Creation of Settings and the Future Societies.* San Francisco: Jossey-Bass, 1972.

———. *The Culture of the School and the Problem of Change.* 2nd ed. Newton, MA: Allyn & Bacon, 1982.

Smith, Frank. *Insult to Intelligence.* New York: Arbor House Publishing Co., 1986.

3

First Viewing

When introducing a poem, instructors usually begin by encouraging students to sit back and enjoy its sounds, rhythm, and language. Later, after sharing their first responses to the poem, students return to it, this time looking more closely.

Similarly, we suggest that teachers simply enjoy their first viewing of the tape and watch it in an impressionistic way. But a brief introduction both to the tape and to the role it will play in the course of study may provide students with a frame of reference.

Overview of the Tape

For example, it may help viewers to know that the teaching episodes occur in the crowded classrooms of the New York City schools. The average class size in most of these school buildings is thirty-five, and it is not unusual for children within one class to speak as many as ten different native languages. The adults in the videotape—Martha Horn, JoAnn Curtis, Shelley Harwayne, and Georgia Heard—are each connected, in one way or another, to the Teachers College Writing Project, which is directed by Lucy Calkins and codirected by Shelley Harwayne.

It will also probably help viewers if they know that the tape is forty minutes long, and that the first viewing will be followed by discussion and perhaps by many subsequent viewings. If viewers will eventually be given a targeted question or topic to discuss, it will probably help them to know this before they watch the tape. Rather than interrupting the tape with questions, participants should be encouraged to jot down their responses and reactions in their notebooks or on prepared viewing sheets (Workshop Materials A). The purpose of these viewing sheets is to encourage viewers to note their responses alongside appropriate places in the video script so that these sections can be replayed during later discussions. Viewers also need to know that if they attend only to the scenes and episodes on the videotape that involve their specific age-level students, they will miss out on many things pertaining to every age group.

In order to encourage teachers to simply enjoy the tape, some workshop leaders downplay the importance of note-taking and discussion topics, and instead bring beer and pretzels to the first viewing. Food and drink may not be crucial, but laughter certainly is. The tape is studded with the humor of children, with the small jokes that brighten classrooms. Humor is an essential ingredient in effective writing workshops, as are teachers' natural, heartfelt responses to children and their writing.

When Only One Viewing Can Be Arranged

If the group of participating teachers can only view the tape once, beer and pretzels can probably be replaced by pen and paper. Viewers might jot notes in two columns, one titled "What I Am Learning" and the other "What I Need to Know" (Workshop Materials B). Or they might record what surprised them or their questions. In either instance, workshop instructors might give viewers a few minutes to reread their notes and circle the major points that seem especially significant before launching into whole- or small-group discussions.

Then, too, if people can only watch the tape once, instructors may want to divide them into small discussion groups and assign a particular topic to each group member. For example, one person from each group might pay special attention to the issue of conferring while another could watch for ideas on classroom management. During the discussion time, each member of the group could lead the discussion on his or her new topic. The topics could echo those in this guide or they could be chosen by the workshop instructors or by the participants.

A third alternative would be to divide the class into interest groups and to give each group the responsibility for teaching the class about one topic. For example, the reading-writing people would watch the tape with their topic in mind, do some background reading, and report back to the class. If the topics explored in this way are those covered in the guide, each interest group could use the guide as a resource.

Selected Readings

Emig, Janet. "Literacy and Freedom." In *The Web of Meaning: Essays on Writing, Teaching, Learning, and Thinking*, edited by Dixie Goswami and Maureen Butler, pp. 171–78. Upper Montclair, NJ: Boynton/Cook Publishers, 1983.

Murray, Donald M. "The Writer's First Reader: Teaching the Other Self." In *Learning by Teaching: Selected Articles on Writing and Teaching*, pp. 164–72. Upper Montclair, NJ: Boynton/Cook Publishers, 1982.

4

Reasons to Write

Although "The Writing Workshop: A World of Difference" is a documentary on methods for teaching writing, in watching the video it is easy to forget that it is about a teaching method and to see it as simply about children, about their voices and their lives.

Effective methods of teaching writing are transparent. What shines through in this videotape and in these classrooms are the children, speaking in voices which are startlingly honest. This is the power of writing.

As Calkins says, "When we share writing, we uncover and share who we are. Writing invites us to put ourselves on the line, to bring ourselves into classrooms, into the teaching-learning transaction. And that has made the world of difference."

When we hear Moira, Richard, Jeter, and the others speak, when we see them cluster together over their writing, the voices seem so natural that it is easy to minimize the challenge involved in turning classrooms into writing workshops. The first and most crucial task is to issue young people that same "generous invitation" that must also be issued to teachers. Young people need to be invited to put themselves on the line, to bring themselves into the classroom, to use writing for their own important purposes.

Investment in Writing

The most powerful scenes in the video are probably those in which we glimpse the personal power writing has in the lives of these young people. Viewers will sense a compelled feeling in the four scenes showing children writing to frame selected moments of their lives: to find, to cherish, and to share personal meanings. Viewers will also sense the vulnerability of these young writers and the trust they have placed in each other.

- 0019–0108: Richard says, "I write to get a lot of madness out of me . . . I can share it with the whole world in a book, but I can't share it by shouting."
- 0149–0160: Marisol reads from her poem entitled "Father." "I wish you didn't have to go to work. I wish you could stay at home and play with me. . . ."
- 0957–0964: Moira tells us about her fear of sharing. "I was thinking that the kids were going to say, 'Boo.' "
- 0974–1036: The closing scene. Erica says, "I wanted to get the words out of me but I just didn't, and I kept them inside me. . . . Let me tell you something. Never lose your courage to tell someone you love them."

It is important for viewers to notice that in these classrooms, students write not only to understand and share their lives, but also for all the reasons that people the world over write. They write to apply for jobs, to twist arms, to protest, to argue for a cause, to plan an event, to teach others. In the videotape, there are examples of this real-world, functional writing:

- 0161–0177: Jeter writes a thank-you letter to author Elizabeth Levy.
- 0074–0098: Adults write to plan for and record the construction of a building, to issue parking tickets.
- 0631–0652: Shuh-Hung tells Martha Horn that he has written several books on trains because he wants to teach his friends about trains.
- 0578–0630: Schallon writes a shopping list, then hangs it on the door of the refrigerator.

In a classroom that is filled with purposeful writing, not all of the writing is published or posted. In fact, purposeful writing is often disposable writing. The videotape is filled with examples of writing on the track of an idea, of writing-to-learn:

- 0135–0149: Personal narratives can be regarded as seeds for other genres, as in Luis's narrative story about cockroaches.

- 0117–0134, 0135–0149, 0149–0160: Lucy Calkins and several children mention the concept of taking the "seed idea" of one story and seeing in it the potential for another story.
- 0192–0212: Writer Georgia Heard free writes at the typewriter.
- 0317–0324: Vinnie documents the behaviors of the class guinea pigs and learns that McCloskey kept similar notes on ducks.
- 0375–0391: Hilary writes an idea down on the tissues she keeps beside her bed.
- 0310–0316: Kindergarteners keep records of their chicks' growth.
- 0653–0700: Shelley Harwayne suggests that Alex take notes on sleep.
- 0767–0801: Shelley Harwayne suggests that Mary jot down things she wonders about.

PROBES

Leaders of a course of study on the teaching of writing may simply want to replay or recall these scenes on the tape and discuss them in general ways with students. If they wish to probe them, however, there are a number of issues they might want to raise.

Choosing Topics That Matter.   Until recently, we would have explained the children's heartfelt investment in writing by saying that young people care about writing when they have the opportunity to choose their own topics. But we have found that even self-chosen topics can be trivial ones and that even deeply important topics can be handled in trivial ways. In many classrooms, students who once cranked out little ditties on assigned topics such as "My Summer Vacation" are now cranking out equally perfunctory pieces on topics such as "When I Went to My Aunt's House." The scenes in this videotape, then, invite viewers to reflect on the enormously complicated and significant issue of student investment in writing.

Encouraging students to write about the topics that matter most to them is probably the first step in helping students care about their writing. In order to do this, teachers need to know students' areas of expertise. Don Graves often begins workshops on the teaching of writing by asking teachers to list the names of their students and beside each name, the child's areas of expertise. How important it is to notice which names are the last ones to be remembered and which children do not have established areas of expertise. It is also important to scan the list of children and ask, "Do these youngsters regard themselves as classroom experts on these topics?"

We can help students develop confidence in their topics if we ask them to teach us what they know. The teacher of writing is a student of students. Listen to Donald M. Murray's description of his teaching:

I am tired, but it is a good tired, for my students have generated energy as well as absorbed it. I've learned something of what it is to be a childhood diabetic, to raise oxen, to work across from your father at 115 degrees in a steel drum factory, to be a welfare mother with three children, to build a bluebird trail . . . to bring your father home to die of cancer. I have been instructed in other lives, heard the voices of my students they had not heard before, shared their satisfaction in solving the problems of writing with clarity and grace.

I feel guilty when I do nothing but listen. I confess my fear that I'm too easy, that I have too low standards, to a colleague, Don Graves. He assures me that I am a demanding teacher for I see more in my students than they see in themselves.

I suppose he is right. I do hear voices from my students they have never heard from themselves. I find they are authorities on subjects they think ordinary . . . Teaching writing is a matter of faith, faith that my students have something to say and a language in which to say it.

(Murray 1982, 157)

The writing teacher takes lessons from students and in doing so, helps them know what they know. Topic choice becomes a much easier proposition when children have confidence in their own information.

Rethinking the Reasons and the Routines for Share Meetings. If viewers replay the scenes cited earlier in this chapter and ask "What accounts for the compelled quality in these episodes?" they may notice that in each episode the writing is *for someone*. It is important for our children to have audiences for their writing.

In many writing workshops, each day's session ends with the whole class gathering to hear two or three students' work in progress. During these "share sessions," children often sit on the floor and the author usually sits in a designated "author's chair." Authors introduce their pieces by briefly commenting on where they are in the process of writing and on the kind of response that would help them the most. After reading the piece, or a portion of it, the author calls on classmates for their comments.

If viewers are familiar with the work of Calkins, Graves, Atwell, and Giacobbe, they will be familiar with the notion of share-meetings. They may not realize, however, that as these share-meetings become institutionalized, they sometimes become rote and clichéd. In some classrooms, the audience follows a prescribed routine. For example, the listeners may begin by retelling the author's piece. Then they ask small questions to clarify or extend the content of the piece. Both of these ways of responding to writing can be helpful, but there are countless other equally valid ways of responding to writing. Two of them are illustrated in the video when Richard shares his poem, "Stallions" (0889–0908). Here, JoAnn Curtis asks students to talk with a neighbor about Richard's poem before raising their hands to share their comments with Richard. Then she asks them to again talk with a neighbor, this time in order to find a question they could ask Richard that would lead him to describe his process of writing. In the videotape the children ask, "What made you decide to write this as a poem?" but they could have also asked, "What problems did you run into while writing this?" or "What discoveries did you make while writing this?" or "Did someone give you wise help while you were working on this poem?"

There are many other ways to target the share session toward a new concern. The teacher could ask listeners to tell the author the words they especially remember from the piece of writing or to give the author a sense of how the piece of writing made them feel. Alternatively, the teacher could focus the sharing by asking readers to share examples of surprising, fresh language, or of language that seems clichéd and needs to be rewritten. Or the teacher could ask each child at the share meeting to give a single sentence that conveys the focus of his or her piece of writing. Still another option would be for children to share their own revision processes and the questions they have about revision.

Then, too, share sessions can be revitalized if we realize that writers need experience writing for a broad variety of audiences. A teacher might divide her class into small sharing groups and arrange for these groups to meet every Friday afternoon with a parent volunteer, a custodian, a "cafeteria-lady," or a librarian. Another teacher might encourage students to send their writing to an aunt in Kansas, a friend in another school building, a favorite author. Another teacher might divide the children into small sharing-clusters such as the one we see at the end of the tape.

Above all, the videotape, and especially the final scene, serves as a reminder that the most important thing is that writers receive genuine and varied responses to their work.

Materials That Encourage Purposeful Writing. If students are writing for a range of purposes, it makes sense for the writing classroom to have a wide variety of paper and writing tools. Viewers may want to replay the scenes that show functional writing, and make a list of the tools, paper, and utensils students can use to accomplish their purposes. Such a list would include small spiral notepads, clipboards, graph paper, poster board, stationery, marker pens.

Responses That Encourage Purposeful Writing. Teachers can help students view writing as purposeful not only by altering the ways we motivate writing but also by altering the ways we respond to it. The best response to a piece of writing is one that fits the purpose behind the piece. Frank Smith has said: "Writing is for stories to be read, books to be published, poems to be recited, plays to be acted, songs to be sung, cards to be sent, cartoons to be labelled, instructions to be followed'' (Smith 1983, 566).

Viewers may note that Frank Smith did *not* say writing is for hanging on bulletin boards, for pasting into photo albums, for framing in Lucite frames. Each of these forms of publication, however, appears in the video-tape. Since the tape was filmed, those of us in the Teachers College Writing Project have begun to question whether there aren't more natural forms of publication available.

The larger issue, of course, is that ideas on teaching writing are always changing. We all need to pull back often, rethinking our own methods of teaching. Viewers may want to search the tape for other messages that need to be revised or extended. Then, too, they can be encouraged to look with the same critical eyes at their own teaching.

ACTIVITIES

Time Lines of Growth in Writing. Each teacher could be asked to jot down a time line of his or her growth as a writer, marking significant moments on the time line. Then the course instructor might say, "As you think back over the time line of your life as a writer, when (if ever) have you felt like a writer? What was it about that time (or those times) that made you feel so connected to writing?" If teachers wrote and then discussed their answers, they could begin to think through their own reasons for caring about writing. Many of them would probably discover that the topic and the audience for their writing had a great deal to do with their investment in it.

Brainstorming Ways to Increase Student Investment in Writing. There are many variations on this activity. Workshop participants could capture their lifelines as writers onto the time lines and then circle and discuss the moments of greatest significance or the turning points. They could chart and analyze the rising and falling of their interest in writing. All of these activities have the potential to produce very important insights about teaching writing.

"How do I get my students to care so much about their writing?" some teachers will ask after viewing the videotape. There are few bigger, more important questions that can be asked. Participants could wrestle with the questions in pairs, in response groups, or as a whole group. The difficult thing about the question, of course, is that every aspect of teaching writing can either *add to* or *subtract from* students' willingness to invest themselves in writing. Participants may want to divide themselves into small groups and then have each group rethink one aspect of the writing workshop.

One cluster of people might consider ways to begin the workshop in order to invite this sort of investment right from the start. They might suggest, for example, that several weeks before launching the workshop, a teacher could begin raising anticipation for the upcoming writing workshop. The teacher might do this by calling youngsters together, circling a date on the calendar, and telling them that on that day they would begin a very special endeavor. In preparation for the first day of the workshop, children could meet in response groups to discuss areas of expertise. They could talk through several possible pieces of writing, learn procedures for the writing workshop, and begin to collect their tools and materials. Above all, they could listen to and learn from wonderful writing, both by professional authors and by children from other classrooms. All of these activities would implicitly convey to these young writers that the writing workshop is a crucially important time.

Another cluster of teachers might discuss ways in which the physical layout of the classroom can encourage children to invest themselves deeply in their writing. These teachers might suggest, for example, that a good writing classroom needs to be filled with children's projects: with maps of summer trips, pictures of family members, collections of rocks and shells and stamps.

In a similar manner, clusters of teachers could examine every aspect of the writing workshop, looking for ways to support student investment in writing.

Highlight the Need for Purposeful Writing. If the teachers viewing the videotape are already leading writing workshops in their classrooms, a number of small staff development activities might highlight the need to add more real-world, purposeful writing to their workshops. For example, if teachers listed the kinds of writing that someone touring their classroom would see at that moment, the lists would probably contain personal narratives, poems, and fiction. If, alongside this, teachers listed the kinds of writing they themselves had done over the past week, the list would probably be comprised of very different genres: memos, plans, letters, instructions. The disparity between classroom genre and real-world genre could also be illustrated if teachers contrasted the writing they had in their possession—in pockets, purses, briefcases and so forth—with the writing their students probably have in their possession during a writing workshop. Both of these activities might lead to a discussion about the need to add more real-world writing to writing workshops.

Strategies for Finding Topics

Textbooks and laminated skill cards often devote many pages to prewriting activities. They may suggest that students fold their papers into three columns, title the columns "people," "places," and "things," and brainstorm possible topics under each category. They may provide students with magazine pictures and follow with open-ended questions such as "What does this remind you of?"—all meant to elicit possible writing topics.

Although these activities are sometimes fun for students, they do not provide young people with the strategies that writers the world over use to find topics for writing.

Tom Newkirk, a professor at the University of New Hampshire, recently suggested that the great teachers in our lives are those people who offer us invitations to be insiders in a field of knowledge. One way to invite young people to be insiders in the field of writing is to help them see that prewriting and topic choice do not happen as a writer sits at the desk just prior to writing. Instead, a writer's whole life is involved in the search for topics. Just as a photographer sees potential pictures everywhere, so too, writers go through life saying, "I could write about that." The writer sees a curious image, hears a new phrase, notices a pattern in events, recalls a moment of poignancy and power . . . and all of these are potential topics.

Our students will rehearse for writing as they read, as they go through the events of their lives, as they interact with friends, and even as they doze off to sleep if they write regularly enough to get into their stride as writers. The first five minutes of the tape are studded with references to these natural sorts of rehearsal. Specifically, the video shows:

- 0192–0212: Poet Georgia Heard talking about how her topics for writing come from something she sees on the street, from previous pieces of writing.
- 0358–0374: Calkins describing possible sources for topics and explaining that predictable, regular writing times encourage students to write when they are not writing.
- 0375–0391: Hilary talking about rehearsing for writing. As she goes to sleep, she writes her ideas on the tissues beside her bed.

Rehearsal, then, does not necessarily involve its own set of special activities. It is more apt to occur through a reflective overlay that is superimposed on the ongoing events of one's life.

There are times, however, when writers *do* engage in activities that are meant, specifically, as ways to find and refine topics for writing. Some of these activities are shown or discussed on the videotape:

- 0302–0314, 0432–0436: In these and other segments, youngsters return to early drafts of their writing, viewing them as seed beds for future writing. "We need to teach children that good topics are not used up." As Calkins says, "We each have only a few seminal issues in our lives and these are like quarries from which we can mine a huge variety of pieces."

- 0279–0309: Good topics are contagious. Calkins emphasizes that children get topics from one another and suggests that encouraging children to move about the classroom as a researcher might, documenting what their friends are writing about, can help youngsters find ideas for writing. Similarly, children can get ideas in classrooms where topics are recorded on a huge chart that contains each child's name and a list of finished pieces.
- 0767–0801: Mary is stuck; she has nothing to write about. Shelley Harwayne suggests that she borrow a strategy from author Kathryn Lasky.

PROBES

Major Revisions Become Rehearsal.   When children reread their personal narratives and see in them the potential for travel writing, memoirs, character sketches, and the like, viewers may question whether it is accurate to label this as rehearsal for writing. "Isn't this revision?" they may ask. The question, of course, is a good one and can be used to initiate a discussion on how the "stages" of writing are recursive and overlapping. It is often impossible to separate rehearsal from revision.

It is also significant to notice that in these instances, topic choice occurs not only when the writer first approaches a subject, but also later, once the writer has begun to work with the material. Sculptors are fond of saying that their subject emerges from the material, and this is also true for writers.

Disposable Writing.   Viewers may notice that in order to select and hone their topics, writers do a great deal of disposable writing. They jot notes, make lists, do research and sketch out plans. There are layers upon layers of writing in a writing workshop.

Beyond Topic Choice.   It is important to stress that rehearsal for writing involves more than choosing a topic. Donald Murray estimates that he spends 75 percent of his writing time on rehearsal. Yet in many writing classrooms, once students learn to select topics easily they spend almost no time on rehearsal.

It may help to share and discuss Virginia Woolf's description of her writing process: "As for my next book," she says, "I am going to hold myself from writing it until I have it impending in me: grown heavy in my mind like a ripe pear or pendant, gravid, asking to be cut or it will fall."

Viewers may also benefit from knowing that Kafka had one word over his desk: "Wait," and that William Wordsworth talked of the writer's "wise passiveness."

When Writers Can't Find Topics.   Viewers may notice that when teachers help youngsters find topics, they do so by giving the youngsters strategies to use whenever they are "stuck." They do not suggest possible topics but instead help students discover methods for finding their own topics. The methods shown on the tape are not the only possible ones. Teachers could have suggested that youngsters do some free writing, refer back to journals they have kept, or brainstorm lists of possible and impossible topics.

Topics with Potential.   Viewers may notice that twice, when talking about topics, Calkins speaks of *good* topics. "Good topics are not used up," she says, "Good topics are contagious."

Instructors may want to emphasize that for any given youngsters, some topics have a great deal of potential while others do not. The challenge is not to come up with a topic but with a *good* topic.

ACTIVITIES

Anticipate and Address Concerns over Topic Choice.   Teachers who have been using more traditional methods of teaching writing may be reluctant to give students responsibility for choosing their own topics. They may voice their hesitations in a range of ways. One teacher may ask, "If every student is writing on a different topic, how can I provide a motivating activity for twenty-five different topics?" Another teacher will say, "I always give my students options. They can either use the story-starter kit, use the topics I provide, or choose their own. It is up to them." A third will say, "But I want writing to be integrated into the curriculum. If we go on a field trip, read a story together, watch something out the window, doesn't it make sense for everyone to write on that topic?"

The workshop instructor needs to anticipate questions like these and be prepared to respond to them. In order to do this, the instructor may want to read pp. 1–12 and 175–83 in *The Art of Teaching Writing* and chapters 3 and 8 of Graves's book, *Writing: Teachers and Children at Work*. More than this, the workshop instructor needs to listen carefully to teachers' questions and ask, "What are the concerns and convictions that underlie these questions?"

Oftentimes teachers are hesitant to relinquish their role as creators-of-topics because they believe that devising wild and wonderful topics is one of the few things they know how to do in the teaching of writing. It would probably help to talk openly about this issue.

Then, too, teachers may have given their students "free choice" on one or two occasions and can probably recall students pleading, "Do we *have* to choose our own topics?"

These are honest and important concerns, and it may help if teachers have the opportunity to delve into them in whole- or small-group discussions. One structured way to do this is to pass out sheets of paper describing the kinds of problematic situations that may arise when students are given the opportunity to select their own topics. A sample sheet containing several such situations is provided in Workshop Materials C and discussed in Workshop Materials D, but it would be vastly preferable if the situations arose directly out of participating teachers' concerns. If teachers turned in log entries or in-class writing about their concerns over topic choice, the instructor could use these to create a list of situations similar to that in Workshop Materials C.

Bring Home the Issues of Topic Choice. One way to help teachers internalize information on topic choice is to ask them to spend time working on their own pieces of writing. "Write on whatever matters to you," the course instructor might say. Later, teachers could discuss their varied responses to an assignment they so often give to students. Then, too, as the course instructor moves about the room conferring with teachers about their topics, the instructor can demonstrate methods for developing topics. And again, the strategies used in these conferences could later serve as topics for discussion.

Research the Relationship Between Topic Choice and Writing Development. In *The Art of Teaching Writing,* Calkins tentatively suggests that the issues surrounding topic choice may change as youngsters grow older and/or more experienced as writers. Workshop participants may want to reread chapters 5 through 11 of *The Art of Teaching Writing* to discover portraits of children-as-authors at each grade level. Here they will find, for example, the suggestion that kindergarteners rarely decide upon their topics for writing in advance. Just as a child will pull back from playing with blocks and announce, "This is going to be a tower," or "I'm making a garage," so too, a child will pull back from drawing and announce, "This is my cat. This is two cats and they are going to marry."

When the first or second grader begins to experience writer's block, it is often a sign that the child is planning his or her writing and anticipating an audience's reaction to it. For the first time, topic choice can become a source of anxiety. It is not uncommon, as Calkins notes, for second graders to write on the same topic over and over again, or to write on topics their friends or the authors of their reading books have chosen.

In the upper elementary school and junior high years, it is especially crucial for some youngsters to feel that their writing adds up to something important. The junior high school child who has written several personal narratives may prefer to view these separate pieces as chapters within an autobiography.

Once the workshop participants have gathered together the information from *The Art of Teaching Writing* that pertains to topic choice, they may want to conduct small classroom-based case studies in order to explore their own sense of the emerging issues surrounding topic choice. They can gather data by interviewing and learning from children at several grade levels, and by studying children's writing folders and writing processes. Later, as they study the data for patterns, they can ask, "Does this match what Calkins suggested we might find? Does my data suggest new trends and issues?"

Selected Readings

Calkins, Lucy McCormick. *The Art of Teaching Writing*. Portsmouth, NH: Heinemann, 1986. Chapter 1.

———. *Lessons from a Child: On the Teaching and Learning of Writing*. Portsmouth, NH: Heinemann, 1983. Chapter 4: pp. 24–29.

Graves, Donald H. *Writing: Teachers & Children at Work*. Portsmouth, NH: Heinemann, 1983. Chapters 1–3.

Murray, Donald M. "Write Before Writing." In *Learning by Teaching: Selected Articles on Writing and Teaching*, pp. 32–39. Upper Montclair, NJ: Boynton/Cook Publishers, 1982.

———. *Write to Learn*. New York: Holt, Rinehart & Winston, 1984. Chapters 1–3, pp. 3–84.

Smith, Frank. "Reading Like a Writer." *Language Arts* 60 (May 1983): 558–67.

5

The Structure of a Writing Workshop

When we think of child-centered education, we often envision a "free" environment, one filled with lots of noise and motion, with students racing from one cluttered work area to another. In the child-centered writing workshops in New York City, however, we have learned that youngsters need responsibility as well as choice. Choice does not need to be accompanied by chaos. In order to enjoy both choice and rigor, students and teachers need a classroom that is highly structured.

It may seem surprising to hear writing process people talk of structure, a word more often associated with traditional classrooms where neat rows of desks face the teacher at the front of the room, who assigns workbook pages to students. This, of course, is not what we mean by a structured classroom. In a writing workshop, the structure is more like that in an artist's studio, a researcher's laboratory, or a scholar's library. Each of these environments is deliberately kept simple in order to support the complexities of the work in progress. They are deliberately kept predictable because the work at hand is so unpredictable.

In the writing workshop, both the schedule and the expectations are also simple and predictable. Students can become strategic, planful learners because they know when they will be writing, which supplies will be available, and what their writing time will be like.

Likewise, writing workshop teachers can step back and understand what's happening to their young writers if they are freed from the demands of constantly choreographing and managing the workshop. When the schedule and routines are well designed, children do not need to ask, "What do I do now?" "Where's the stapler?" "What do you mean, edit?"

When teachers first turn classrooms into writing workshops, they need to think about the use of time, space, and materials. Time is probably the most essential of these three resources. The teachers in the video, knowing that students cannot do their best if they write only once or twice a week, have set aside long and frequent blocks of time for writing—an hour a day four or five times a week. Teachers at the junior high school level who need to teach literature and language skills within one fifty-minute English period, however, cannot give this much time to writing. Instead of holding the writing workshop once a week throughout the year, these teachers cluster the time they have for writing into concentrated units so that, for at least a time, their students write daily.

It is critical that students know about the predictable schedule so that they can plan for their writing time, rehearsing at home like Hilary on the videotape.

Just as it is essential to have lots of time for writing, it is also important that within each writing hour, the time is well-used. Viewers will probably see that the teachers in the video have divided their writing hour into several component parts.

Most of these teachers begin their daily workshop by gathering students together and teaching them something about good writing. This ritual, sometimes called a mini-lesson and sometimes an author's meeting, lasts only a few minutes, and is generally followed by a workshop in which students work on their current pieces of writing and confer with their teacher and peers. The writing hour often ends with the entire class meeting to respond to several students' work in progress.

Staff development instructors who decide to replay certain scenes from the videotape to highlight the workshop's component parts might view the following:

- 0445–0473: The mini-lesson on writing mysteries.
- 0574–0578: The scene in which students work on a range of writing-related tasks, while their teacher, JoAnn Curtis, walks about the room, conferring with students.
- 0889–0908 Richard reading his finished poem to his friends, who have gathered together for a share-meeting.

The teachers in the video have also given a great deal of thought to the use of classroom space. By pushing desks together into clusters and leaving pathways between the clusters, they have made a physical commitment to the importance of talking and movement in the writing workshop. By making tools and materials accessible to youngsters, they have freed themselves from tasks such as dispensing paper and sharpening pencils, and can instead devote themselves to conferring with students. Each teacher has also created a place for whole-class meetings. One did this with a fringed area rug, while others have left a patch of floor space open.

Viewers may want to study the backdrop of each scene in the videotape, for although these urban classrooms do not have the space or furniture available in many suburban schools, the teachers have used classroom space in deliberate ways to support the writing workshop. If viewers want to study specific scenes, it may help to return to the same three scenes that illustrated the use of time:

- 0445–0473: During the mystery mini-lesson, children sit on a large striped rug placed at the back of the room. The teacher's chair and the author's chair are both placed at the front of the meeting area.
- 0574–0578: As the teacher begins to move about, conferring with students, she has the space necessary to move between tables and to crouch alongside individual writers, working with one at a time.
- 0889–0908: Children have returned to the striped rug. This time JoAnn Curtis pulls her chair alongside "the author's chair." JoAnn's position next to Richard enables her to help him guide the discussion.

Then, too, the teachers in the video recognize that tools embody a philosophy. "Scissors, staplers, and Scotch tape help students view early drafts as tentative," Calkins says. "File boxes filled with cumulative folders encourage students to save and honor their messy drafts." Viewers will be able to compile a long list of writing tools as they look at each scene of the video. They will see a variety of kinds of paper, and they will notice that, although these are overcrowded urban classrooms, there is nevertheless space for children's own interests: these classrooms are rich in animals, plants, teacher and student collections, and shared projects. Good writing classrooms are filled with people's lives.

A few scenes seem especially relevant to a discussion on the tools and materials for writing:

- 0392–0409: Georgia Heard describes her tools. Her list includes a cumulative file of poems, her stack of papers, her favorite books, her typewriter.
- 0302–0309, 0432–0436, 0709–0733: These three scenes illustrate some of the ways we can use a student's cumulative writing folder: folders can be a source of inspiration for future writing; the pieces in them can be reviewed, ranked and evaluated; and the finished personal narratives can be treated as seedbeds for new modes of writing.

- 0212–0216: A child compiles a list of possible topics, which is stored in her daily writing folder.

Much of the teaching in a writing workshop involves designing predictable, ongoing structures and then redesigning these structures in response to changing needs. The teacher of writing needs to step back periodically to ask, "What's working that I can build on?" "What's not working that I can fix?"

If children's energy for writing seems to have plateaued, the teacher may add new materials: blank books, big reams of computer paper, marker pens. If the classroom feels cramped during writing time, the teacher may study traffic patterns in the room searching for bottlenecks. As a result, the teacher may decide to dispense with the supply center and instead put a basketful of supplies on each cluster of desks, or divide daily writing folders into three piles and store each pile in a different corner of the room.

The predictable structure in a writing workshop will change in response to identifiable problems, but it will also evolve in response to new topics of study. For example, the teacher who is about to begin a study of poetry may set up a special table and each day, bring to it treasured anthologies of poems. This teacher may also leave blank books alongside the anthologies and invite students to search for and copy down their favorite poems to create their own private anthologies.

Several scenes in the video demonstrate the ways in which new topics of study influence the ongoing structures in a writing workshop.

- 0045–0473: At the end of her mini-lesson on mystery writing, JoAnn Curtis invites children who have been reading in this genre to meet at a special table to discuss reading-writing connections.
- 0317–0324: Clipboards are among the tools in this workshop. Here a young boy uses a clipboard as he observes the class pet so he can weave true bits of information into a fictional piece.
- 0653–0700: Spiral notepads are among the tools in this workshop. After his conference, Alex is given a spiral notepad to assist him in taking notes on the sleeping habits of his family.
- 0161–0177: Beautiful stationery, kept alongside the other writing paper in Jeter's classroom, has encouraged Jeter to write a letter.

PROBES

Planning for a Writing Workshop. When teachers establish a writing workshop in their classrooms, they create a community, a culture, a way of life.

In order to plan for this sort of teaching, teachers need to think about the use of time and space, the availability of tools, and the role of ritual. What a different sort of planning this involves than that called for in traditional lesson plans!

There's No One Way to Teach Writing. Instructors may want to reassure viewers that, although the teachers in this video have structured their writing hours in similar ways, this does not mean that these are the only ways to organize writing workshops. A colleague of ours, Pat Wilk, compares the component parts of a writing workshop to modular furniture: you select the pieces that are important to you and then shuffle them about, rearranging them in ways that work best for you. The writing workshop might include these components:

- A teacher-directed meeting, sometimes called a mini-lesson or an author's circle.
- An in-class writing session. Sometimes a portion of this time is reserved for silent writing. Usually children know they may confer with each other or with their teacher during writing time.
- A share-session. Writers share work in progress and receive help from their peers. The teacher monitors and participates in share-sessions and uses this time to model methods of peer conferring.
- Alternative forms of share-sessions. In some classrooms, children share their writing in pairs or in groups led by parent volunteers. In other classrooms, children disperse throughout the school to share their work with secretaries, librarians, and the like.
- Response groups. Youngsters meet regularly in small groups to hear each other's work and to confer with each other. Generally, the response groups take the place of share-sessions.
- Seminars. Sometimes in-class writing is set aside and a full hour or a full week is devoted to in-depth study of a topic.

These are not the only possible components of the writing workshop. Others are invented by teachers in response to the needs of a particular class. There is no one correct way to structure the writing hour. One teacher may want to begin each writing workshop by calling students together for a discussion (mini-lesson) on good writing. Another teacher may find that silent reading is a natural pathway into writing. Still another may ask youngsters to spend the ten minutes prior to writing in response groups or free writing in their logs. The important thing is that a teacher doesn't attempt to do all of these, each on a different day. This would put the youngsters in the position of constantly waiting to discover their teacher's changing agenda.

The Predictable Structure and the Rules That Undergird the Writing Workshop. Underlying the videotape and the teaching it depicts is the belief that classrooms need to be structured in simple and predictable ways. This means, of course, that teachers need to design activities that last not only for a day but for the entire year. It also means that young people deserve to know that these activities will continue for a long while.

In an effective writing workshop, young people should be able to explain the components of the workshop. They should know when writing time will begin and end, how long a share-meeting will last, what happens to finished work. Young people should also know their teacher's expectations and the rules that govern life within the writing classroom.

Viewers can replay the video to search for evidence of the rules that are probably in effect in these workshops. They may notice, for example, that when children come to the meeting area, they do not carry pencils, paper, toys, or gadgets with them. Viewers will also notice that when children gather for class meetings, they are asked to sit on their bottoms rather than kneeling on the floor. When children confer with each other during the writing workshop, they usually do so on the edges of the classroom, and they speak in soft voices. Viewers will see evidence of these and many other rules throughout the videotape.

Convey Respect for Tools and Materials. Viewers may suggest that children need rules to govern the use of materials. It is certainly true that the workshop can fall into chaos if rough drafts aren't stored in folders, if scissors and Scotch tape aren't returned to the supply center, if students forget their pencils and pens.

Rules, however, are not always the most effective way to govern what happens in a writing workshop. Expectations can be conveyed in other more positive and natural ways.

For example, children will respect their materials when the workshop is conducive to respect. Daffodils on the editing table and a lace tablecloth under the book display table will convey more than any list of rules.

Select Tools with Care. In *Notebooks of the Mind,* Vera John Steiner suggests that tools shape inquiry. Viewers will see that certain tools are essential in any writing workshop. These include daily writing folders for work in progress and cumulative writing folders for finished work. But these "folders" need not always look like folders. Students in some classrooms have been known to use grocery bags for work in progress or to hang their unfinished pieces on a clothes line. They have used large manila envelopes or shoe boxes for finished work.

Viewers will see other tools, as well. What they may not see, however, is that by including additional, carefully chosen tools, teachers can influence what happens in a writing workshop. Viewers should be encouraged to imagine a writing workshop in which children worked with Polaroid cameras, video recorders, tape recorders, periodicals, double-entry logs, survey sheets and the like.

The Reading Table. If the structures of a writing workshop are meant to embody a philosophy of teaching, then it makes sense for teachers to find particular ways to embody their commitment to reading-writing connections. The round table, mentioned in passing in the videotape is one way to do this. If students are involved in writing research reports, the round table might contain stacks of *National Geographic* magazines. Through mini-lessons or activity cards, students choosing to work at the round table might be encouraged to notice the titles of articles, contrasting those in the *National Geographic*, such as "Mexico: An Alarming Giant," with the more generic labels they generally use for their own research reports.

Similarly, students writing poetry might study the ways other poets use white space, search through poems for examples of surprising language, or notice how published poets title their poems.

ACTIVITIES

Reflect on the Hubbub of the Writing Workshop. During the hectic pace of the school day, teachers rarely have an opportunity to step back and reflect on the strengths and weaknesses of their workshops. It might be helpful, then, to provide teachers with a chance to distance themselves from the hubbub of the classroom by doing some free writing on their workshop arrangements. In particular, they might think about the trouble spots that occur during the writing workshop. If teachers have not yet begun their workshops, they can try to anticipate the problems that might arise.

Instructors might begin by saying, for example, "As I take you through the writing time, I'll mention some of the activities your class might be doing. As I do this, try to picture the scene in your classroom and jot down any trouble spots." Then the instructor could begin by saying, "The students are finishing their math period, and it's time to stop and begin writing workshop. You are asking students to get ready to meet you at the front of the room for a short author's gathering. [Pause.] The students are sitting in front of you as you begin to give information." [Pause.] Each pause reminds people that their task is to envision the workshop and to anticipate the problems that may be occurring. The instructor could continue, "Your short lesson is over and you want the pieces students are writing currently to be distributed." And the instructor would proceed in this manner, giving time throughout for teachers to jot down their concerns. Later, the workshop instructor could ask teachers to look over their notes and identify the trouble spots that might be eliminated by changing room structures, routines, or materials. The teachers could then chat in small groups about how to make these changes.

Draw a Floor Plan. Teachers may find that many of their problems are related to their use of space in the room. If students are cramped into a tight space, they may become fidgety and quarrelsome when they gather for a share-meeting. If students must move tables and chairs, the noise volume in the class often gets too high. If supplies for the entire class are kept at the center of one cluster of desks, students seeking supplies will probably disturb the writers who are working there.

It might be helpful, therefore, to ask each teacher to draw a floor plan of his or her classroom, and then, working with a partner, to design the best arrangements for a writing workshop. By talking this over with a colleague, teachers may realize they have more options than they had realized for arranging desks and for designing areas for supplies, conferring, editing, and publishing.

Classrooms That Convey a Respect for Craftsmanship. In *The Art of Teaching Writing*, Calkins suggests that teachers can raise the standards of their students' writing by creating a gracious, beautiful setting conducive to craftsmanship.

Workshop instructors might suggest that teachers read pp. 213–16 in this text and then meet in grade-level groups to brainstorm about some of the little touches they could add to their classroom environment. Teachers could do this for several areas in the room, including the classroom library, the storage area for writing folders, the editing table, the supply center, and the students' desks.

Classrooms Reflect Changing Priorities. When teachers are interested in exploring a new frontier in the teaching of writing, it makes sense for them to begin by getting their classroom ready for the new work. To consider the ways a classroom can be changed in anticipation of a new topic of study, teachers could form small task forces, each one selecting a genre that they might want to bring into their workshop. These small task forces could then search for literature to add to their libraries, find reference texts and articles that they might want to have on file, decide on special writing supplies they might need, and develop new means of publishing children's writing.

Selected Readings

Atwell, Nancie. *In the Middle.* Upper Montclair, NJ: Boynton/Cook Publishers, 1987. Chapter 3.

Calkins, Lucy McCormick. *The Art of Teaching Writing.* Portsmouth, NH: Heinemann, 1986. Chapter 4, pp. 23–29; chapters 17–19, pp. 163–94.

———. *Lessons from a Child: On the Teaching and Learning of Writing.* Portsmouth, NH: Heinemann, 1983. Chapter 5.

Graves, Donald H. *Writing: Teachers & Children at Work.* Portsmouth, NH: Heinemann, 1983. Chapter 4.

6

Early Writing

One of the most exciting things happening across the country is that young children are writing sooner than we ever thought possible. Teachers are no longer waiting until children can form letters perfectly, read at certain grade levels, recite rules of syllabication and spelling, or label parts of speech, before inviting them to be insiders in the world of written language. In fact, during the very first weeks of kindergarten, when handed a beautiful blank book and a marker, very few children say, "I can't write."

Of course, their early attempts are pages filled with houses and mountain peaks and labeled with squiggly lines and random strings of letters and numbers. Early childhood teachers are marveling at these early efforts because they have come to appreciate that learning to write is a developmental process not unlike learning to speak.

When a baby's first attempt at saying "doggie" sounds like "dah" we don't correct the child's pronunciation or worry that the child has speech problems. Instead, we delight in these early attempts and respond, "Yes, that's a doggie."

In the same way, when the young child fills her pages with the loops and squiggles of "pretend writing" and announces, "It's a story about my kitten," her teacher draws her chair in close and celebrates the youngster's intentions, her willingness to approximate, and her potential as a fledgling writer.

As children begin learning a few initial consonant sounds, their teachers will see that their invented spellings become closer and closer approximations of adult writing. The teachers' responses continue to be filled with acceptance and gentle nudging. They trust that when young children label rainbows "RNBZ" and dinosaurs "DNSRZ" the children are writing as best they can. Teachers also trust that children's writing will fill out as the year goes on. This will be evident, for example, in the case study of Dwayne (Workshop Materials E). Invented spelling is incomplete, not incorrect.

Workshop instructors might take a moment or two during the showing of the videotape to watch the faces of the viewers. The scenes of very young writers will probably be the ones that make the audience smile and shake their heads in disbelief. Viewers will be charmed by the beauty and the endearing sincerity of very young writers, by their seriousness and their interest in learning to write.

Schallon writes *macaroni* on the class shopping list and believes that this list is exactly what the make-believe kitchen needs. John, whose random strings of letters tell of a butterfly carrying people from a burning building, believes in this magic. The children who so eagerly pitch in to spell *morning* for a friend are devoting their full attention to this important work because they know the author needs to complete his treasured picture book.

These scenes are very special ones and deserve to be replayed several times.

After viewing these scenes, teachers will readily see that young children can write if we help them. And we can provide the kind of help children need if we understand what is unique about very young writers.

The first issue that sets our youngest writers apart is the role their drawings play in their writing processes. This is an important issue throughout the case study of Dwayne (Workshop Materials E). Often young children's drawings become an integral part of their topic selection. For example, a child might begin drawing and then decide that the picture reminds him of the sun coming up. The child might then announce that he is writing a story about waking up in the morning. In this instance, the drawing serves as rehearsal for his writing, although it is not the same purposeful, planful rehearsal that older students will do. For the very young writer, the act of drawing and the picture itself both provide a scaffolding within which the piece of writing can be constructed. The child draws, then writes, then draws some more. Each new drawing nudges the child to add more to the written text.

Young children's drawings are themselves unique because we can often see developmental breakthroughs as we study them. Four- and five-year-olds often scatter isolated objects across their papers: a boy, a house, a sunflower. If they do any writing at this time, it is usually labeling the objects, much like the pages in a picture dictionary.

Teachers delight when the child first adds a groundline to the picture, because the drawing now has more of a story to tell. The boy is walking behind his house and planting seeds for more sunflowers. Squiggly or dotted lines are used to show the boy's arms bending down to plant the seeds. Then, too, the boy may now appear in profile. This author's effort to invent ways to represent action in the pictures is not unusual. When pictures represent stories, the writing tends to be a narrative rather than a label. Children often write a sentence underneath each picture, and with help, they begin to follow one picture with another, one sentence with another.

A second characteristic of young writers is that their revisions tend to involve adding on. They write a little bit, and especially if they're surrounded by an interested audience, they then add more information to their stories.

Teachers often find that their job involves helping young writers learn different ways to make space for additional information. Some primary-age children enjoy writing new pages and stapling them onto their first, one-page draft. In this way, pieces of writing become books. Often children prefer to tape new sheets of paper onto the bottom of their initial page, creating scroll-like stories. Then, too, primary-age children can learn to discern when they have left important pieces of information out of the middle of their texts. With help, they can learn to use arrows to insert the missing information.

Children of this age group, however, do not tend to write multiple drafts of a piece. Nor do they usually use the range of revision strategies that one might find in an upper-elementary class. A teacher can introduce revision strategies to these youngsters, however, and almost any strategy can be simplified enough to be applicable to the primary grades. For example, when six-year-old Steven writes:

My grandmother is a great cook
It's fun at her house

his teacher might say, "Imagine Steven, that you're going to share your writing with all the other students in the class. You're going to sit in the author's chair and read your story aloud, and then the children will have a chance to ask you questions. Steven, why not read your story to yourself right now and try to guess what questions your friends will probably ask when you share. You could even jot them down and we can chat about them." In this way, Steven begins to revise his writing so that it answers his reader's questions.

Viewers may want to come up with other ways to help young children feel at home with revision strategies. First graders can learn to rearrange pages, to divide long texts into smaller pieces, to make their written text more exciting, to rewrite a piece in a different genre, or to turn a story into a picture book. Further information on this can be found in chapter 7 of *The Art of Teaching Writing*.

But perhaps the most unique characteristic of young writers is their wide repertoire of spelling strategies. Young children often do not derive their spellings from visual memory as adults tend to do. When children first begin to break the code, to link sounds to symbols, they often do so by matching the sound of a letter's name to the sound the child is trying to capture in print. This explains why, when Shuh-Hung writes his train book, he spells *track* "HRK." The letter *h* ends with the /ch/ sound that almost matches the /tr/ sound Shuh-Hung needs to spell *track*. Similarly, many young writers use *y* for /w/. "We take a walk" might be spelled "yetakayak." Sometimes names of letters take the place of whole words. "You are my friend" might appear as "U R mi Frd."

Young students also rely heavily on consonant sounds, often hearing just the initial sound. *Computer* appears simply as "K." When they hear final consonants as well, *computer* now appears as "KR." As they learn to say words slowly, stretching them out to hear even the medial consonant sounds, *computer* might then be spelled "KPTR."

There are three scenes in the videotape that illustrate young writers' spelling strategies. These scenes represent points along a developmental sequence. John's random string of letters about his butterfly represents an early stage, followed by Schallon's efforts to spell *macaroni*: with her teacher's help, she says the word slowly. Finally, a cluster of children help one another tackle the difficult word *morning*.

- 0124–0278: Martha Horn's interest in John's picture of a big butterfly and a house that is blowing up leads John to tell—and to create—a story that links components of the picture together. When Martha tactfully suggests that John might write a word or two, the youngster tells her that he has already done so and produces a page full of print. The writing appears to be a random string of letters. Undaunted, Martha asks John to read the story aloud. John tells a tale about zebras, not worrying that the length of the story corresponds to the length of the print or that the content is consistent with his previous version. Martha Horn celebrates what he has done.
- 0578–0630: Martha Horn helps Schallon complete a class shopping list. The child wants to write *macaroni*. It would have been very easy for Martha to have dictated the correct letters, but instead she helps the young writer spell the word on her own. "Watch me, watch my mouth," Martha says, and then invites the child to join her in slowly articulating the sounds of the word. The close-up of this young speller illustrates well how much attention young children pay to the feel of the position of their lips, tongue, and teeth.
- 0474–0502: A cluster of children, and specifically a young girl, eagerly help a friend spell *morning*. The scene reminds us of how important it is to arrange desks to allow for this kind of interaction.

In addition to viewing the scenes that pertain specifically to the early grades, workshop instructors will want their primary teachers to study the entire tape, because every section of the tape has implications for very young writers.

Our early childhood students have much in common with students of all other ages. For example, five- and six-year-olds can do what Alex, the fifth grader, does to research his family's sleeping patterns. They can carry memo pads in their overalls and take notes on their baby brothers, their cocker spaniels, or even the way acorns fall from the oak tree in front of their apartment building.

So too, young children can write thank-you letters to visiting authors as twelve-year-old Jeter has done, as well as take part in a wide range of real-world writing. Kindergarten children delight in writing their own absence notes, taking inventory of lost and found items in the classroom, or labeling the plants in the school corridor.

It seems then, that most of the strategies and activities we offer our older students can, in some way, be offered to our younger writers. So too, young children can do what Luis has done and take the seed of a personal narrative and turn it into other genre. First graders write about baseball games they've played in, and from these personal narratives they can go on to write how-to books on baseball, or poems about being on the winning team.

PROBES

Workshop instructors may decide to replay the entire videotape and ask viewers to think through the implications of each scene for K–2 students, or they may decide to replay only those scenes that are unique to our youngest writers. In either case, the following issues may be probed.

Elicit a Story from a Drawing. Martha Horn brings out John's story with the question, "What's happening?" and with the expectation that the picture represents a story. John probably would have produced only a label had she asked, "What is it?" instead of "What's happening?"

Encourage Children to Move from Drawing to Writing. In the same scene, viewers will notice the way Martha Horn turns John's attention from drawing to print by asking, "If you were to write something about this story. . . ." Then she lets John know that writing even one word would be acceptable by saying, "If you were going to write one thing, one very important thing. . . ." Viewers may want to hypothesize different ways the conference could have gone if John had not already done an entire page of writing. If John had chosen to label his picture with just one word, "volcano,"

Martha probably would have done what she did in the macaroni scene. "Vol-ca-no. Say it slowly. What sounds do you hear?" If John sounded out the initial *v* sound but did not know which letter to put on the paper, Martha might have taken the opportunity to show him how to use the illustrated alphabet chart hanging under the chalkboard, or she might have invited the children sitting nearby to pitch in as they do in the morning scene. On the other hand, the child might have listened to the *v* sound in volcano and then announced, "I hear a *g*." Martha would then have invited him to put that letter down, despite the fact that it was the "wrong" letter. Later, Martha would try to figure out the logic in John's decision, and she might teach him the correct sound-symbol correspondence.

Use the Drawing for Context Clues. Workshop instructors may want to discuss what would have happened if, in the same scene, Martha had asked John to read his text, and John had responded with, "I don't remember," or "I can't read." Martha might then have peered at the letters, trying to figure out what they said and inviting John to help her do so. After this she probably would have referred John back to the drawing. "I bet your words tell about what's happening in your picture . . ." she might have said. Martha knows that a text contains many meaning clues, and she uses all of them to try to find the child's meaning. Meanwhile, she demonstrates that reading involves much more than decoding letters.

Teach Spelling Strategies. Viewers will notice the ways these children develop strategies that help them become independent. After Martha sounds out *macaroni*, she invites Schallon to do it for herself. In this same scene, the child seems to have lost her place in sounding it out. "Another *k*?" she asks. Instead of simply correcting her, Martha shows her how to get back on track by referring back to the text and inviting the child to reread what she has written so far. In this way Schallon finds her place in sounding out.

The Issue of Spelling Errors. Teachers may wonder if allowing children to use a *k* in *macaroni* leads to bad habits in spelling. This is an important issue, and workshop instructors will probably want to refer them to the articles in the bibliography.

ACTIVITIES

Refer to Recommended Readings. Many fine articles and texts have been written about young writers, and workshop instructors will no doubt suggest that viewers do some of the recommended reading. They might also want to divide the group into reading clusters and distribute copies of an article to the members of each cluster. It would be important to provide time for cluster members to share their reactions to the readings and to decide how to teach the larger group about what they had learned from the article. If the course will be meeting over a long period of time, teachers might reread the same article at a later date and again discuss it in the same response groups, but this time they could also discuss how their reactions to the article have changed over time.

Bring Children into the Staff Development Sessions. So often, when we share information about young writers, teachers wonder whether such growth can really happen in their own classrooms. They are often skeptical about whether their youngsters could really produce pieces of writing like those they see on the videotape. Instructors, therefore, might plan to hold a workshop in a school building at a time when kindergarten classes are in session. They might give each teacher blank books and a can of marker pens and send each off to work with a cluster of children.

During this activity, instructors could move among the teachers and children, showing teachers ways to help children make the transition from drawing a picture to writing about it.

They should be sure to schedule time for teachers to meet together afterwards to talk about what they noticed.

Simulate the Classroom. If it is not possible to visit classrooms, instructors might simulate an early childhood writing workshop by asking half the group to take on the role of students. They might then give each "student" a piece of writing and a little slip of paper with background information about the writer.

For example, one student writing sample might contain only an elaborate drawing. The slip of paper might say, "You're a verbal five-year-old who loves to tell stories that go with your drawings. You know some initial consonant sounds, but you are hesitant to use them; therefore you do not write any words to accompany your picture." Or, accompanying a piece filled with pretend-writing, there might be a slip of paper saying, "You do not know any sound-symbol correspondences, but you are perfectly content to 'read' your story for as long as the teacher is willing to listen."

Other situations might include the following:

- The child who is comfortable with invented spelling but forgets what the words say, and whose spellings are cryptic enough that the teacher cannot decode them.
- The child who always writes one sentence about his picture and does so quickly and easily. He does not seem to know what to do once he has written the sentence, and so he bothers his classmates.

- The child who copies her spelling from a poster on the back wall.
- The child who continually asks the teacher for spelling help.

Case-Study Research as the Centerpiece in Staff Development. The case study is a particularly effective means of inviting teachers to appreciate young children's growth as writers. Instructors might, therefore, also want to involve teachers in a case-study research project that spans the length of the course. Teachers could each pick one child in the class to watch. They might also want to develop a set of questions to ask every few weeks in order to note the child's growth. The set of questions might include:

- What do you have to do to be a good writer?
- How do you go about spelling hard words?
- What's the best piece you've written? Why is this the best?

Teachers can learn methods of case-study research from Glenda Bissex's, *GNYS At Work,* or from Lucy Calkins's, *Lessons from a Child.* If teachers are unable to conduct case-study research projects, instructors could ask them to bring in a young child's cumulative writing folder, making sure pieces are dated, or they could use Dwayne's folder, which has been included in Workshop Materials E.

In either case, there are several ways to interact with the pieces of writing teachers bring to the workshop. Instructors could turn one set of pieces into overheads, and the teachers could discuss the changes they notice in a particular student's writing over time. Or instructors might find it preferable to make a copy of one child's pieces available to each workshop participant. Then, in small groups, teachers could investigate different areas of growth. For example, two could study evolving spelling strategies, two could examine drawings, two could look at punctuation, two could look at the emerging awareness of audience.

An Early Childhood Videotape. Workshop instructors might be interested in acquiring another videotape, this one dealing exclusively with the early childhood years, which was produced by the same team that made "The Writing Workshop: A World of Difference." Although it was done in a hurry, many people find it very valuable. It is entitled "Our Youngest Writers" and can be purchased from the New York City Board of Education. Those who are interested should contact Nola Whiteman, New York City Board of Education, 131 Livingston Street, Brooklyn, NY 11201 (phone number: 718-596-3888).

Study and Observe Children's Spelling Strategies. If teachers are interested in exploring some of the finer points of young children's spelling strategies, a good place to begin is with Tom Newkirk and Nancie Atwell's article,

"The Competence of Young Writers," in *Perspectives on Research and Scholarship in Composition*.

After discussing the article, teachers might want to do some "kidwatching" in their own classrooms. Instructors might suggest that they each pick just a few children and then, with clipboard in hand, spend a few minutes each day observing what the children do as they spell. When teachers share their findings with other workshop participants, they will probably notice that some children ask their friends for help, some rely on the alphabet chart, and some peek at picture dictionaries. With closer observation, teachers will notice those children who pay close attention to the position of their lips, tongue, and teeth as they stretch words out, and children who rely heavily on letter names and consonant sounds; they will also see children who have begun to use their visual memory of words.

To give teachers additional practice in appreciating students' spelling strategies, a selection of young children's writing appears in Workshop Materials F. Teachers can be asked to guess the spelling strategies these young children probably used as they wrote. Comments on these samples are provided in the section "Reflections on the Spelling Strategies of Our Young Writers" (Workshop Materials G).

Selected Readings

Bissex, Glenda. *GNYS AT WORK: A Child Learns to Write and Read*. Cambridge, MA: Harvard University Press, 1980.

Calkins, Lucy McCormick. *The Art of Teaching Writing*. Portsmouth, NH: Heinemann, 1986. Chapters 5 and 6.

Harste, Jerome; Woodward, Virginia A.; and Burke, Carolyn L. *Language Stories and Literacy Lessons*. Portsmouth, NH: Heinemann, 1984.

Kamler, Barbara. "One Child, One Teacher, One Classroom: The Story of One Piece of Writing." *Language Arts* 57 (September 1980): 680–93.

Newkirk, Thomas. "Archimedes' Dream." *Language Arts* 61 (April 1984): 341–50.

Newkirk, Thomas; and Atwell, Nancie. "The Competence of Young Writers." In *Perspective on Research and Scholarship in Composition*, pp. 185–202. New York: The Modern Language Association of America, 1985.

Sowers, Susan. "Six Questions Teachers Ask About Invented Spelling." In *Understanding Writing: Ways of Observing, Learning & Teaching*, edited by Thomas Newkirk and Nancie Atwell, pp. 47–56. Portsmouth, NH: Heinemann, 1986. (Originally published in 1982 by The Northeast Regional Exchange, Chelmsford, MA.)

7

Conferring: The Heart of the Writing Workshop

Almost half of the videotape focuses on responding to student writing, and it is right that this is so. The teacher of writing has two essential challenges: to establish a richly interactive workshop environment and then to move about within it, responding to children and their writing.

Janet Emig recently told the story of an elementary school principal who went into a writing workshop to observe the teacher. For a moment he stood in the doorway, glancing around the room. One youngster worked at the chalkboard, diagraming the sections of his volcano report. Nearby, three children clustered to hear act 2 of Jorge's play, "The Missing Egyptian Pearl." Other children worked at their desks, some scrawling furiously on pads of legal paper, and some carefully copying their work onto white paper. Occasionally one of them would turn to read a line or discuss a point with a classmate. On the edges of the classroom, children met in twos, listening to each other's pieces. In the far corner, three or four children worked at a table full of dictionaries. Finally the principal spotted the teacher, who was sitting alongside one student in the midst of the workshop. The principal made his way across the room to where she sat and, leaning down, said, "I'll come back when you are teaching."

How little he knows about the challenge of teaching writing well. The teacher who sits beside a youngster, responding to writing in process, is involved in an enormously complicated and demanding aspect of the writing workshops.

In most summer institutes and in-service courses on the teaching of writing, the bulk of time is devoted to the questions that surround the issue of conferring:

- How do I respond when a child comes to me, draft in hand, saying "I'm done"?
- How do I help youngsters become critical readers of their writing?
- There are so many ways in which the children's writing is inadequate. Which aspect do I address in a conference?
- How do I motivate the students to do their best work?

Conferring is a difficult skill to develop because there is no way to patent and repeat a successful conference. Each conference is an entirely new event with its own particular combination of ingredients and constraints. A teacher needs, above all, to be responsive to whatever emerges in a conference. It is easiest to do this if the teacher brings to the conference a deep and broad knowledge of writing development, the qualities of good writing, and effective writing strategies. Above all, however, the teacher must rely on his or her knowledge of that particular child.

In the Teachers College Writing Project, we have struggled with the issue of how to help teachers improve their ability to hold productive writing conferences. At one point, we wondered if it would help to demythologize conferring. We wondered if, instead of simply saying that teachers must listen and respond, we needed to give teachers specific guidelines. In *The Art of Teaching Writing*, Calkins suggests that conferences can be loosely categorized as process conferences, design conferences, content conferences, or evaluation conferences, and she discusses each one.

It has been clear to us, however, that although it helps to analyze and dissect effective conferences, it helps even more to demonstrate effective conferences. For this reason, much of our staff development work with teachers involves demonstration teaching, in which we work with children in classrooms while teachers observe. But we have found that sometimes observing teachers feel all the more insecure when they watch effective conferences. As they watch, they are often thinking that they would not have responded to the youngsters in that particular way. "How did you know the right thing to say?" they ask. It is important for us to stress, therefore, that there is never one single approved script for an effective conference. But while there are hundreds of different, equally good ways to respond to a student, some conferences are more effective than others, and several principles underlie effective conferences.

What these principles are is not entirely clear. Certainly one of them is that effective conferences are filled with natural talk: with exclamations, jokes, suggestions, ideas, feelings. Probably another is that in an effective conference, the writer learns something that will help him or her another day with another piece of writing. Donald Murray once suggested that the single most important guideline for effective conferring is that the writer must leave the conference wanting to write. The writer's energy should go up, not down.

Those who view the videotape will suggest other guidelines for effective conferences, and those who have read the work of theorists in the teaching of writing will report on their espoused principles. The important thing, of course, is for the teachers in our workshops to recognize that we are, all of us, continually engaged in redefining the elements of good teaching. Viewers must develop, and then critique, their own ideas on topics such as conferring.

Almost every segment of the videotape can be used as a reference during the staff development sessions that are devoted to this topic. Information on the characteristics of good writing relates to the subject of conferring as does information on reading-writing connections, rehearsal strategies, and reasons to revise. The most obvious lessons about conferring, however, can be learned from those sections of the videotape that allow viewers to see teacher-student and peer conferences:

- 0124–0278: Martha Horn encourages John to tell the story of his volcano picture and suggests he do an accompanying piece of writing. She then learns that John has already written a string of letters that represent the story he wants to tell. John reads these to his teacher.
- 0503–0548: Three seventh graders discuss one boy's story. The author's friends are not sure that the details of the story are clear.
- 0578–0630: Martha Horn helps Schallon add *macaroni* to her shopping list. The child then posts the list on the door of a toy refrigerator.
- 0631–0652: Shuh-Hung has written many books on the topic of trains. His teacher asks why he has written so much on one topic. "It's a teaching story. . . . If someones don't know about trains, then the teaching book will teach them."
- 0653–0700: Shelley Harwayne hears that Alex thinks his research report on sleep is too boring, so she recommends that he gather data on his subject matter through interviews and observation.
- 0709–0733: Farah has finished her piece of writing. "This is one of my favorites," she says to her teacher. Her teacher tells Farah that after completing a successful piece of writing, it is often helpful to reread it, studying to see what worked well in it. The teacher goes on to recommend that Farah try ranking all her recent pieces from best to worst.
- 0734–0766: Andrew is writing a book with chapters, so he and his teacher look together at a published book that follows a format similar to the one he will use.
- 0767–0801: Mary has no ideas for a writing topic, so Shelley Harwayne suggests that she borrow Kathryn Lasky's strategy of writing in order to explore the things she wonders about.
- 0802–0856: In one of the greatest episodes on the videotape, JoAnn

Curtis tries to encourage young Salvatore to focus his piece of writing. "I'm wondering . . . is there one, most important thing?" she expectantly asks. "No," Salvatore says, and then assures her, "I could write even more." She tries again. "Could you take a minute and look it over. See if you could find just *one* idea that . . ." "That what?" he asks, totally bewildered by the implications of her question. "That you like," JoAnn says, losing confidence. "I like *all* of them," Salvatore responds, and the conference continues in this way.

- 0857–0888: Two girls talk together about the problem one of them is having trying to turn her narrative into a play.
- 0974–1036: A cluster of children respond authentically to Erica's heartfelt piece about her great-grandfather's death.

PROBES

Conferring Changes Once the Workshop Is Well Established.   The episodes on the videotape were filmed after students had spent seven months in writing workshops. When the workshop first begins, teacher-student conferences more closely resemble the peer conferences on the videotape. Teachers move about the room, learning what their students know and helping students trust their own areas of expertise.

When we show this kind of interest in our students' lives and in their stories, children begin to write with more detail and more authority. They also become effective audiences for each other, expressing interest and confusion, responding with sincerity and curiosity.

Once students are responding to the content of each other's pieces, teachers can devote more of their energy to reflecting upon and extending the processes students use to write.

Myths of Conferring.   A close look at these conferences may help viewers challenge some popular myths about conferring. These include the notion that in a conference, teachers ask the writer questions.

Questions can be important in a conference, but it is a mistake to believe that in an ideal conference, teachers always ask a barrage of small questions. Teachers also muse out loud, repeat what they have heard, make suggestions, explain their ideas, share knowledge, respond emotionally to a story, give tentative assignments.

When teachers do ask questions, some of them are tiny questions meant only to help a child continue his or her line of thinking. Other questions are major ones that suggest new lines of inquiry, and one or two of these are far more valuable than fifteen.

More Myths of Conferring.   Another popular idea about conferring, which the video challenges, is the notion that in a conference a writer's problems are solved. Often, a conference ends when a problem is identified, not solved. "Why don't you work on that," the teacher may say as she leaves the child. Alternately, the teacher may say, "That might be a possibility. Why don't you give it a try?"

A third myth the video challenges is the idea that in a conference, writers teach us about their subject matter. This happens in some conferences, but viewers will find that in these episodes, it is equally common for writers to teach us about their writing processes, their ideas on good writing, their attitudes towards writing, their plans for a draft.

New Ideas on Teaching Writing Affect Teacher-Student Conferences.   Viewers will notice that teachers refer to children's literature in many of the conferences on the videotape. This should illustrate for viewers that those of us in the Teachers College Writing Project see literature as a crucial resource in the writing workshops. But viewers should also know that literature happens to be a very big concern to us at this particular time, and that every new idea on the teaching of writing affects our conferences. For example, in our staff meetings we have recently been thinking that children need to realize that there are real-world reasons to write. This idea, like every other idea in the teaching of writing, has implications for conferring. If a teacher postpones speaking with a youngster about publication possibilities until the draft is completed and selected as one of the youngster's very best, then the youngster misses out on the opportunity to write the piece with specific readers and purposes in mind. Published writers tend to pull back from their writing early on and ask, "What might I do with this piece?" "Who is it for?" These are the big questions that, if asked early on in a teacher-student conference, can transform both a draft and the process of writing that draft.

The child who is writing about how his grandmother gave him twenty dollars might become newly invested in the piece if he views it as a thank-you letter. The youngster who is writing fiction may want to turn the story into a Big Book and give it to the kindergarten class. The student who is writing about a cousin who died of a drug overdose may want to submit the piece to a drug prevention writing contest. In each instance, it helps for teachers to ask questions such as, "Who is this for?" and "What will you do with this draft after you finish it?"

The larger issue is that a teacher's ideas on conferring must continually change because whatever new topics become important to the teacher will influence how the teacher conducts teacher-student conferences.

Critiquing the Videotaped Conferences.   There are several ways in which the videotape necessarily misrepresents our ideas on conferring. First, in the tape there are many more teacher-student conferences than there are peer conferences; in reality, the reverse is true. Then too, in the videotape the normal contingent of onlooking children, hovering around the edges of a teacher-student conference, is not evident. None of the conferences shown last fifteen seconds, as many do in a writing workshop, and if the conferences refer back to earlier mini-lessons (as they often do), viewers who haven't seen the mini-lessons will not be aware of this.

Each Conference Occurs Within a Context. Some viewers will find it disconcerting that when Farah finishes reading her story about her baby brother, JoAnn Curtis says only, "I can see why you love the story," before she goes on to suggest that Farah rank all of her pieces from best to worst.

"Why doesn't JoAnn respond to the content of the piece?" viewers may ask, and the question is a reasonable one. It is true that in most instances, teachers begin by responding to the content of the piece. This is especially true if the student has read the piece out loud in the conference.

Yet viewers also need to remember that any one conference takes place within the context of other conferences. JoAnn Curtis may have heard the piece of writing on the preceding day and spoken with Farah then about her baby brother.

Viewers also need to realize that teachers do not always need to talk with writers about the subject matter of a piece. It is easy to talk so much about baby brothers, cockroaches, fishing trips, and motorcycles that we do not talk about criteria for evaluating writing, strategies for revising a piece, or plans for future writing.

Writing teachers should respond not only to the writer's subject matter but also to the writer's goals for writing, opinion of a text, attitude toward writing, outlines and plans for a draft.

The conference with Farah shown on the videotape will pave the way for a later discussion about what makes one piece of writing better than another. JoAnn Curtis will eventually respond to Farah's sense of good writing and to her methods of evaluating her writing. This discussion may (and may not) lead Farah to generate ideas on how to improve her story.

Revision of Teaching. Viewers should probably know that the teachers on this videotape are not satisfied with their conferences. In afterthought, they see many ways to improve each of them. In part, they report that it was disconcerting to have a video camera, two cameramen, two coproducers, and a director hovering around as they conferred. Martha Horn feels that as a result, she did not extend the children's writing as much as she often does. Shelley Harwayne is convinced that Alex and Mary were unusually quiet and self-conscious. It is probably true that the conferences would have been more effective had the conditions been more natural, but it is also true that for all of us, our conferences are rarely "perfect." The important thing is that we are willing to stand back from our teaching and critique it, learning from what we have done.

Viewers can probably suggest ways to improve on each of these conferences. Hopefully, they can also suggest ways to improve on each of their own conferences.

The Importance of Audience. The videotape, and especially its final scene, serves as a reminder that writers need genuine and varied responses to their work.

Teachers may want to reflect upon ways we can provide our young writers with a wide range of audiences. For example, upper-grade students might regularly read their picture books to "kindergarten partners." Students might make monthly visits to a neighborhood senior citizens' center to share their work with an "adopted grandparent." Junior high students might share a collection of stories about their school with graduating sixth graders. Young poets from throughout the school may organize a poetry reading or publish an anthology of poems.

ACTIVITIES

Categorize Teacher-Student Conferences. Viewers may want to read chapters 12 to 16 in *The Art of Teaching Writing* because they discuss writing conferences. Viewers might then consider which of the videotaped conferences illustrate each kind of conference described in the book. It would be important to emphasize that these categories are just one way of talking about conferences; there are no clear-cut distinctions between each kind of conference, and there are undoubtedly many other ways to categorize writing conferences.

Still, it may be helpful to see that JoAnn Curtis's discussion with Farah can be classified as an evaluation conference and that Martha's talk with John about the giant butterfly and the fire is a content conference. It may also be helpful to think of Shelley Harwayne's conferences with Alex and Mary as process conferences.

Role-Plays That Illustrate the Guidelines for Effective Conferences. Oftentimes it helps to introduce the topic of conferring by asking people to divide up into pairs. One member of each pair becomes the teacher, the other the student. Those who agree to role-play the part of students raise their hands and a draft of writing is passed out to each one. As they read their drafts, they each take on the identity of the author. Then each "student" turns to the person who is role-playing the teacher and announces, "I'm done." (This process of creating an identity around a draft is illustrated in Workshop Materials H. The identities created there could be used by staff development leaders.)

The teachers know they are to talk to the writer in such a way that the writer learns something about writing. After a few minutes, the course instructor warns people that they need to finish up the conference.

When the role-played conferences are completed, the course instructor may want to briefly review some guidelines for effective conferences and then ask people to return to their partners in order to process the conference, discussing ways it could have been improved.

The course instructor will want to draw upon what he or she knows and believes in order to devise the short list of guidelines. The instructor may also want to refer to Calkins's guidelines (*The Art of Teaching Writing*, chapter 12) or to Donald Murray's guidelines (see Workshop Materials I).

Learning to Shorten Conferences. There are interesting and helpful ways to vary the activity described above. For example, the course instructor may want to send all the "teachers" into the hallway and ask the "students" to spread out among the desks in the classroom. The "teachers" are then told that they have ten minutes to move among the "students," helping as many of them as possible with their writing. (Students must be forewarned that many different people will approach them and that they need to pretend each time that they have not just had a conference.)

After ten minutes, the instructor may want to take a poll of how many conferences the teachers were able to have. "How many of you had *ten* conferences?" "Nine?" "Eight?" . . .

Inevitably, this activity will highlight the fact that teachers tend to spend too long in a conference. If a teacher has thirty students, it isn't practical for each conference to last three minutes. The other students will grow restless, the line of people waiting for help becomes too long, and the workshop begins to feel chaotic.

It is easy to say "shorten your conferences" but harder to do it. Here are some suggestions:

- Don't solve the problems of the world in a conference. Instead, treat a conference as a time to share one strategy, to give one tip, or to learn one thing about the writer.
- Notice unnecessary and time-consuming aspects of your conference. For example, do you ask unnecessary questions ("What's the title?")? Do students read their pieces to you? (It is always quicker and usually equally effective if you skim the piece yourself.) Do you always read the piece, the whole piece? (This is often unnecessary.)
- The conferences that tend to be the longest are those that focus on subject matter. Evaluation conferences are quick, as are process conferences.
- Vary the length of your conferences. It helps if a teacher has *some* thirty-second conferences. ("Have you shared this with a friend yet? Why

didn't you?" "Have you reread it yet? That's an important thing to do. Reread it and see what ways you come up with to make it better.") Other conferences can then be long and leisurely.

The activity need not lead into a discussion on the length of conferences. Instead, each "teacher" can simply retrace his or her pathway in the classroom and receive some feedback from each conference partner.

Analyze the Videotaped Conferences.   Viewers may want to replay the conference scenes, asking whether the writer gained a tool, strategy, or attitude that might help another day with another piece of writing. In a good conference, we are teaching not the writing but the writer. If the piece of writing improves but the writer does not learn something that can help another day with another piece, then the conference was not especially effective.

Viewers will probably find that in the *macaroni* scene, Schallon developed her spelling strategies. In Shelley Harwayne's discussion with Alex about his report on sleep, the youngster learned the importance of primary research and developed a tool (a spiral notebook) for doing it. In JoAnn Curtis's conference with Farah, the youngster learned that when she writes well, it is helpful to reread what she had done in order to learn what worked.

Viewers will probably also find instances in which writers did not learn a tool, strategy, or attitude that they could use again when confronted with another piece. The challenge then will be to discover how the teacher could have improved the conference.

Beyond Content Conferences.   In our work with teachers around the country, we have noticed a tendency to talk with students almost exclusively about the *content* of their pieces. "Who won the baseball game?" a teacher will ask. "Did the crowd cheer?" "What did the crowd say when it was cheering?" "How did you feel?"

Questions such as these help youngsters recognize that they are authorities on topics and that the details of their topics are important to readers. But students can ask questions such as these of each other in peer conferences (as we see in the discussion on the mushroom cloud). Teachers of writing need to be willing to talk with students not only about their subject matter but also about their writing.

One way to investigate and dramatize teachers' hesitation to talk about the writing is to display a draft on an overhead projector and ask, "What might you ask the writer of this draft?" The hypothetical questions can be written down and later categorized. Are they questions about the writer's writing process? The writer's opinion of the piece? The writer's purpose?

The writer's problems and concerns? The way this particular draft fits into the writer's development as a writer? The writer's hopes for readers? Or are almost all of the questions about the subject matter itself?

Personal Style and Conferring. Each teacher in the videotape has her own identifiable style of conferring. Viewers may want to try to describe and understand each person's style, think about the problems and possibilities inherent in each one, and think, also, about their own tendencies as teachers. If we can pull back from our own teaching and recognize our tendencies and patterns, then we are able to improve our teaching.

Cross-References to Other Conferring Activities. There are several activities listed in other sections of the guide that also involve conferring. Viewers who are particularly interested in literature will probably want to check the activity in chapter 8 entitled "Weave Author Anecdotes into Conferences," which invites teachers to weave information about authors into their conferences, and the activity in chapter 8 entitled "Conferring with a Book Under One's Arm," which challenges teachers to refer to literature when they confer. Viewers who are early childhood educators will probably want to check the activity in chapter 6 entitled "Simulate the Classroom," in which teachers are asked to role-play and respond to young writers' drafts.

Selected Readings

Atwell, Nancie. *In the Middle.* Upper Montclair, NJ: Boynton/Cook Publishers, 1987.

Calkins, Lucy McCormick. *The Art of Teaching Writing.* Portsmouth, NH: Heinemann, 1986. Chapters 9, 12–16.

———. *Lessons from a Child: On the Teaching and Learning of Writing.* Portsmouth, NH: Heinemann, 1983. Chapter 5.

Graves, Donald H. *Writing: Teachers & Children at Work.* Portsmouth, NH: Heinemann, 1983. Chapter 14.

Murray, Donald M. *Learning by Teaching: Selected Articles on Writing and Teaching*, pp. 164–72. Upper Montclair, NJ: Boynton/Cook Publishers, 1982.

Sowers, Susan. "Reflect, Expand, Select: Three Responses in the Writing Conference." In *Understanding Writing: Ways of Observing, Learning & Teaching*, edited by Thomas Newkirk and Nancie Atwell, pp. 76–90. Portsmouth, NH: Heinemann, 1986. (Originally published in 1982 by The Northeast Regional Exchange, Chelmsford, MA.)

8

Literature:
The Most Crucial Resource
in a Writing Workshop

If I wanted to learn the skills of pottery, I would begin by studying a potter at work. If I wanted to weave baskets, or build a brick wall, I would apprentice myself to the masters of these crafts.

Similarly, if we want our students to learn the craft of writing, we need to help them build apprenticeships with their favorite authors.

In the videotape, teachers have filled their classrooms with stories about authors, and they have lined their classroom shelves with the finest in children's literature. Teachers who view the tape will see that literature is woven into these K–8 writing workshops both through anecdotes about the lives of authors and through the study of wonderful texts.

Stories of Authors' Lives

Seven-year-old Greg announced, "Before I ever wrote a book, I used to think there was a big machine and you type the book's name onto the machine and then it goes until the book is done. Now I know, when I look at a book, that a guy wrote it and it's been his project for a long time."

When children view themselves as authors, as insiders in the world of written language, they gain a new awareness of the authors behind the books on their shelves. Teachers can foster this awareness and channel it into lessons on writing if they know bits of information about the lives and work of favorite authors. Author anecdotes can be the subject of whole-class gatherings (mini-lessons) and they can be woven into writing conferences, as is evident in these sections of the videotape:

- 0767–0801: Mary is "stuck" with nothing to write about. Shelley Harwayne suggests that Mary borrow Lasky's strategy of writing on subjects she has always wondered about.
- 0653–0700: Alex worries that his report on sleep is dull. Shelley Harwayne suggests that if Alex observed people as they slept and interviewed them on their sleep habits, researching his subject as E. B. White researched spiders, Alex could bring new life to his text.
- 0317–0324: In order to write a fiction story, a student carefully observes the class guinea pig. He learned to do this from Robert McCloskey, another fiction writer, who grounded *Make Way for Ducklings* in careful observations. While writing the book, he kept ducks in the bathtub of his Greenwich Village apartment.
- 0889–0908: It is significant to note that in the videotape an eight-year-old author is used as a resource. When Richard completes his stallion poem, JoAnn Curtis encourages his classmates to bring their questions about writing poetry to Richard.

PROBES

Workshop instructors may want to simply replay these scenes, emphasizing that teachers can convert anecdotes about authors into lessons on writing. If they have time, however, they might want to invite the teachers in the workshops to mine the scenes for insights about reading-writing connections. Among other things, they will probably want to comment on these things:

Take Cues from the Writer. In the two conferences cited first, the pattern is similar. First the teacher and student identify a problem the student is having with writing, and then the teacher says something like, "You may want to try a strategy another author used to solve a similar problem." In order to do this sort of conferring, a teacher does not approach the conference planning to tell the student a particular bit of information about an author. Instead, the teacher begins by trying to understand the youngster. As the teacher listens to the child, the teacher thinks, "Do I know another author (a famous one or one from the classroom) who has solved a similar problem in a way that might help this student?" This means, of course, that teachers cannot prepare for these conferences except by learning as much as possible about the lives and craft of authors, and by constantly thinking, "How might this be brought into the classroom?"

Select One Thing to Teach. Although the teachers in the videotape have files full of information on authors, they do not try to squeeze everything they know about an author into one conference. There are other times in the writing workshop when the class works on in-depth author studies; the conference is not the appropriate forum for this. Too much information about an author would take the focus of a writing conference away from the child's writing.

Leave Room for the Writer. There are crucial little ways in which teachers signal to the child that their suggestions are tentative. Instead of assigning strategies, teachers tentatively suggest that a student *may* want to try a strategy. "You might try . . ." they say, "Come and see me if it doesn't work out." Viewers will notice that tone of voice and gestures add to the tentative quality of these suggestions.

ACTIVITIES

Weave Author Anecdotes into Conferences. If workshop participants are each given a sheet containing information on authors, they can then be asked to integrate these author anecdotes into simulated writing conferences. The instructor could take the part of a young student in the role-plays, and the viewers could respond as if they were the classroom teacher, weaving in references to the authors when and if they seemed relevant to the child's writing. (Workshop Materials J elaborates on this idea.)

In order to lead this activity, instructors will need to gather together a collection of author anecdotes (or decide to use those in Workshop Materials K).

After distributing author sheets to participating teachers, the instructor may want to suggest that participants turn and discuss with a colleague how these author stories might be woven into teacher-student conferences.

Then, the instructors will need to think through the identity they will assume in the role-play. Instructors can borrow from those included in Workshop Materials J, but it will probably be more effective if they create the character themselves.

Then, role-playing a particular student who is facing a particular dilemma as a writer (see Workshop Materials J for examples of students), the instructor ("student") says something like "I'm done," or "I don't have anything to write about" or whatever else seems appropriate to the character. In the role-play that ensues, someone from the group joins the role-play as the teacher. In order to get someone from the group to join the role-play in this way, the instructor may need to slip out of the student role for a moment, asking "What might you say to me? Will someone play the part of the teacher?" The first person who volunteers will probably attempt to *discuss* rather than *participate* in the role-play. The person might say, "I would ask you. . . ." If this happens, it helps to coach the volunteer into role-playing by saying something like, "Play the part," or, "Be the teacher."

Generally, it is more effective to maintain the assumed identity through-out one entire teacher-student conference before shifting out of the role in order to discuss it. Also, it is more lifelike if the simulated conference is between the instructor and only one "teacher" rather than a whole classful of "teachers." The person who first volunteers can be encouraged to follow the conference through to the end; only then would a second person try conferring.

If volunteers confer in different ways with the same "student," this effectively illustrates that there is no one right way to weave author stories into a conference. Also, each new conference acts as a critique of the ones before it.

Later, the instructor may want to divide the group into pairs, giving one member of each pair a slip of paper describing the student he or she is to role-play. The other member of the pair becomes the teacher, who then draws not only from the author stories on the sheet but from other author stories he or she knows. Again "teachers" and "students" must be en-couraged to actually role-play their parts rather than abstractly discuss what they might say.

Develop a File of Author Anecdotes.   Teachers will only be able to use author stories as a teaching tool in their classrooms if they have a large repertoire of stories to draw upon. Although it is tempting simply to supply them with these stories, it is probably more helpful to show teachers where they can find their own author anecdotes. An effective workshop activity, there-fore, might be to distribute a variety of articles and books to the participating teachers, and to ask each teacher to search for a story and then to learn it well enough to tell it to the group. A list of articles that would work well for this activity is included in Workshop Materials L.

In the discussion that surrounds this activity, instructors may want to suggest another way to invite students into the process of studying authors. Each student (or each response group) may want to select one favorite author to act as that student's (or that group's) mentor. In order to do this, the student would read everything by the author, relating the texts to the author's life.

Use Author Anecdotes to Introduce New Tools and Rituals.   It might also be helpful to encourage workshop participants to think about effective ways of weaving author anecdotes into the ongoing fabric of life in their writing workshops. The course instructor might tell participating teachers one anecdote and then ask them to speculate about how this anecdote could best be told to children. For example, the instructor might say that Don and Audrey Wood, coauthors of *The Napping House*, collected quotes, anecdotes, drawings, and newspaper clippings in a cardboard box and used that box as a source of inspiration for their stories. Then participants could brainstorm ways to convey this information to their students. No doubt they will suggest telling this anecdote in whole-class meetings or in conferences. The course instructor could then suggest that it would be more effective if a teacher not only told the anecdote, but also used it to introduce similar cardboard boxes into his or her classroom. In this way, the author story could be an embodied presence in the classroom long after it was first told.

Workshop participants might invent similar ways to follow up on other author studies. A list of author stories that suggest new tools or rituals is included in Workshop Materials M, and a discussion follows in Workshop Materials N, but it would be more fun if instructors and participants collect their own.

Using Literature as a Resource for Learning About Good Writing

New York City teachers have always tried to teach their students the qualities of good writing. They used to do this by simplifying these qualities into catchy phrases and presenting them as "tricks" authors use to make their pieces better. Five years ago, it would not have been surprising to find a laminated checklist hanging in a prominent spot in the writing center, filled with reminders such as "Sharpen your Lead," "Prune the Clutter," "Show, Don't Tell." Unfortunately, these labels led to caricatures of good writing. Pieces written by children around the city began to look similar to one another. They tended to begin with catchy leads, with "Wow," "Whoosh," or "Kerplash," and to contain a detailed chronology of one small event in the child's life.

Now, New York City teachers avoid simplifying qualities of good writing into items that can appear on a checklist. Instead, they try to give students a sense of the various tones and textures possible in powerful writing. They do this, above all, by surrounding students with wonderful literature. When students know a piece of literature so well they carry words, phrases, and images from it with them as they write, this guides them. In the video, viewers will see three classroom scenes that illustrate the way teachers use literature in teacher-student conferences and in whole-class gatherings:

- 0445–0473: JoAnn Curtis challenges her students to learn from the mysteries they're reading. She suggests that students study published mys-

teries to learn how professional writers build up a sense of suspense and how they invite readers to participate in solving the mystery.
- 0734–0766: JoAnn Curtis helps Andrew use books from the class library as a resource. Andrew has been struggling with the organization of his "how-to" book, and now he will study the tables of contents in professional how-to books.
- 0325–0357: Richard tells his classmates that he got the idea for his poem about stallions from a book, *Thunder, the Mighty Stallion of the Hill.*

PROBES

Workshop instructors may decide to replay these three scenes and discuss some of their implications.

Students Read and Write Within the Same Genre. It is significant to realize that JoAnn Curtis taught this particular mini-lesson on mysteries because she knows the students and their writing well. She has taken their writing folders home in order to determine what information they need. She does not teach from a sequential list of mini-lessons or from a book entitled *One Thousand Good Writing Lessons*. Instead, her teaching is a response to what she sees in the classroom.

It is also significant that JoAnn Curtis expects that students who are writing mysteries will also be reading mysteries. Students will make connections between their reading and writing more easily if their reading is similar to their writing. When elementary and middle school students read only long paperback novels, this is problematic. Very few of them are writing texts that resemble those they are reading. If students are writing short personal narratives, it may help if they spend some time reading very short personal narratives. Martha Horn has helped us realize that, surprising as it may sound, one place to find excellent examples of short, beautifully written personal narratives is in the picture books that primary school children enjoy. For example, *When I Was Young in the Mountains*, by Cynthia Rylant, can act as a powerful model for upper elementary school writing.

In many writing classrooms, ten- and eleven- and twelve-year-olds search through stacks of picture books, studying authors' uses of detail and the design of their texts.

Maintain a Broad View of Literature. It is also important to stress that when we have a broad view of literature it is easier to parallel what students read with what they write. Students should be reading sports journalism, book reviews, letters to the editor, poetry, speeches, advertisements, and travel brochures as well as fiction. They may keep files with examples of exemplary writing from each of these genres, and these files could become part of a class library. These libraries are crucial: JoAnn Curtis is only able to suggest that a student pore over some how-to books because the class library contains a wide range of books.

ACTIVITIES

Conferring with a Book Under One's Arm.   Martha Horn often begins workshops for teachers who are interested in reading-writing connections by suggesting that they each think of the piece of children's literature they and their students cherish the most. She then asks teachers to imagine that they have tucked that book under their arm as they weave about their classroom and to think of all the ways they can refer to it as they confer with students.

Because workshop participants viewing the videotape will probably not have their most beloved books with them, instructors may want to bring multiple copies of a well-known piece of children's literature to the staff development session. People could then reread a short chapter from, for example, *The Lemming Condition*. Alan Arkin's book begins:

Sunlight streamed into the burrow, landed on the floor, worked its way slowly up the wall, and came to rest on Bubber's face. As it touched him Bubber woke with a start. He sat up, full of anticipation and ready to go.

After teachers have an opportunity to reread the text (or a selected part of it), instructors could display a draft of student writing on the overhead projector and ask teachers to turn to a neighbor and together think through possible ways of weaving references to the literature into their conferences with the student. Depending on the problems and potential in the student draft, teachers may suggest that Arkin's lead could demonstrate that good writing does not need to begin with dramatic action, since he has successfully woven his description of the setting into the action of the story; or they may point out that his lead illustrates the way details can transform a piece of writing—from "Bubber woke up abruptly" to the sentences at the beginning of *The Lemming Condition*.

Instructors might also add literature to the conferring activity entitled "Learning to Shorten Conferences" in chapter 7. This time, when half the teachers leave the room, they might each carry a favorite piece of children's literature with them. The text should be one they know well, so that when they return to the room and begin conferring with the "students," they can weave references to the text into their conferences. In a real class situation, the teacher will probably be most apt to carry around the book he or she is reading aloud to the class, although it is also a wise idea for teachers sometimes to carry around the book they are reading for their own pleasure.

More Ways to Weave Literature into Conferences.   A variation of this activity might be to ask the group who will simulate "teachers" to go into the hallway empty-handed and, while they are in the hall, to ask those who will simulate "students" to put the literature they are reading on their desks along with their writing. Then the instructor can direct teachers to confer with students about their writing and later ask how many of the teachers wove references to the literature into conferences; alternatively, instructors could ask teachers, prior to the conferences, to use the books as teaching tools wherever it makes sense to do so.

Common Problems in Mini-Lessons.   Teachers who are used to forty-five-minute developmental reading lessons often find it difficult to use literature as part of a two-minute mini-lesson. The workshop leader can address this issue by first reviewing chapters 18 and 19 in *The Art of Teaching Writing*. Then the workshop leader can help participants realize that mini-lessons are not the time for thorough discussions of literature. Instead of talking about setting, character, editing, illustrations, and word choice, the teacher chooses a single lesson that can be taught based on the book. In order to choose this one, single lesson, the teacher must think, "What is the one tip about writing that will be helpful *today* for my students and their writing?"

The starting point in thinking about a mini-lesson involving literature is not the piece of literature itself but the children and their needs as writers. This is a radical notion. Instructors can help teachers to understand this by asking them to spend a few minutes thinking about a mini-lesson that involves literature. Most of them will begin by thinking "What book should I teach?" Instructors can then point out that a more appropriate starting point is the question "What are the writing issues my children are struggling with at this point?"

Dramatize the Need to Take Cues from Students.   In order to give teachers a feel for the process of devising mini-lessons on literature, course instructors might schedule a staff development session in the school library or begin a session by wheeling a huge cart full of children's books into the room. Then the instructor might provide time for teachers to read and reread some of the texts, emphasizing that teachers will only be able to use literature as a resource if they know it well.

Instructors might then point out that if teachers simply got into small groups and came up with mini-lessons using their favorite texts, they would be creating out-of-context lessons. The answer to the question, "What do I teach in a mini-lesson?" lies in students' writing folders. Teachers need to be aware of what's happening in their students' writing before they can select appropriate tips about good writing to share.

One way to demonstrate this point would be to pass out a sheet with short descriptions of class writing problems. A sample sheet is included in Workshop Materials O and is discussed in Workshop Materials P. Workshop participants may read, for example, about a situation such as this one:

Your students' writing folders are filled with pieces that summarize the proceedings in the big events of life: birthdays, holidays, trips. You would like students to know that good topics can also involve everyday moments and the little things in life that are important.

Workshop participants can then find a piece of literature that would help teach students the value of the little details in our lives, design a mini-lesson based on that piece of literature, and teach their mini-lesson to the rest of the group. Their colleagues can give them feedback.

Workshop instructors will probably want to consider a few tips on literature mini-lessons for these feedback sessions. These might include the following points:

- There's no need to read the entire text during a mini-lesson.
- Teach only one thing at a time; the book can always be used again as a resource for other lessons.
- Try to avoid reducing the qualities of good writing to labels, such as "focus" or "details" or "colorful language," and instead use many different ways to talk about effective literature.
- It helps to tape-record mini-lessons and listen to the ways you talk about literature. Hopefully your tone and your vocabulary will sound natural, and the discussion will be more like booktalk among adults than a lesson one finds in schoolrooms and textbooks.
- Not only can the same topic be the source of many mini-lessons, but the same mini-lesson can often be given several times. For example, it would be worthwhile to teach students time and again about the importance of anticipating their readers' questions as they write.
- When teachers offer students a strategy, such as listing optional titles for a draft, this strategy will probably pertain to only a handful of students that day. Not all students will need any one piece of information on any one day; rather, the tip will become part of the workshop environment.

Selected Readings

Atwell, Nancie. *In the Middle.* Upper Montclair, NJ: Boynton/Cook Publishers, 1987. Chapters 7–10.

Boomer, Garth. "A Parent's Guide to Literacy: Reflections on Literacy and

Learning." In *Fair Dinkum Teaching and Learning*, pp. 96–167. Upper Montclair, NJ: Boynton/Cook Publishers, 1985.

Calkins, Lucy McCormick. *The Art of Teaching Writing*. Portsmouth, NH: Heinemann, 1986. Section V, pp. 219–57.

Hansen, Jane; Newkirk, Thomas; and Graves, Donald, eds. *Breaking Ground: Teachers Relate Reading and Writing in the Elementary School*. Portsmouth, NH: Heinemann, 1985.

Harste, Jerome; Woodward, Virginia A.; and Burke, Carolyn L. *Language Stories and Literacy Lessons*. Portsmouth, NH: Heinemann, 1984.

Smith, Frank. *Reading Without Nonsense*. 2nd ed. New York: Teachers College Press, 1985.

Spencer, Margaret. "Children's Literature: Mainstream Text or Optional Extra?" In *English in the Eighties*, edited by Robert Eagleson, pp. 114–27. Sydney, Australia: Australian Association for the Teaching of English, 1982. Distributed by Boynton/Cook Publishers, Upper Montclair, NJ.

Trelease, Jim. *The Read-Aloud Handbook*. New York: Viking Penguin, 1979.

Teachers particularly interested in children's literature might want to join the Children's Literature and Reading Special Interest Group of the International Reading Association and subscribe to their publication *The Dragon Lode*. Write the Center for Curriculum and Instruction Elementary/Secondary Education, 118 Henzlik Hall, Lincoln, NE 68588-0355. Teachers will also want to subscribe to *The Horn Book* (31 St. James Ave., Boston, MA 02116).

9

Transcript of the Video "The Writing Workshop: A World of Difference"

LUCY MCCORMICK CALKINS: When I watch children explore what their words can do, when I see them talk about writing with such seriousness and care, I am reminded of why the teaching of writing has become so important to me. I care that our young people use writing to accomplish real purposes, that their writing gets better, but I think all of us care about the teaching of writing especially because it has helped us rediscover some simple old truths, truths which often get lost in the frenetic pace of teaching and testing, competencies and textbooks. Truths like: that the kids are at the heart of our teaching; truths like: that it's good teachers, not textbooks and curriculum, which can make the world of difference. And the writing workshop is a world of difference.

Recent educational reports have shown us that classrooms are often characterized by student passivity, by rows of desks facing forward. How different writing workshops are! Because these classrooms are filled with an active hubbub and yet also with rigor, they've given us a new image of what productive classrooms can look, sound, and feel like. Changes in classrooms have come as we implement radical new ideas on the teaching of writing.

It's amazing that the ideas are radical. Take, for example, the notion

Note: This transcript has been edited for clarity; consequently, it may not always correspond exactly to the voices on the tape.

73

that we need to provide students with occasions to do what real writers do. Of course students need opportunities to write in a natural, real way. The only startling thing is that this is a relatively new notion. When I was in school my teachers tried so hard to come up with creative topics which lured and motivated students to write, but I don't think they very often stopped to ask, "Why do human beings write anyway? What are the real, natural reasons to write?" There aren't many real, natural reasons to write "My Life as a Pen," or "The Day I Was a Waterfall." Sometimes these creative topics were kind of fun to write about, but I don't think they helped me discover the real, human reasons to write.

In our classrooms we can help youngsters to realize that beneath all those layers of fear and resistance so many of us have towards writing, there are reasons, real human reasons, to write.

We write to record, and to plan and organize our lives. Some people write to organize other people's lives. We write to play with words and to marvel in what we can do. We write on the job: designing, sequencing, recording. But most of all, we write to make sense out of our lives.

JESSE: When I write, I get a lot of madness out of me. Like if something happened to me, or in my family, I can write about it instead of shouting out. Because I can share it with the whole world in a book, but I can't share it by shouting. Everybody'd just get an earache.

DAVID: Most of my ideas come from things that happened and I take those ideas and I combine them with other things, and together I come up with this mass idea, and I write it down. And it kind of flows, one thing after another until I get used to it.

LUCY CALKINS: Just as David takes the seed idea of something that happened to him and makes it into a mass idea, so too, many of our young writers in New York City take the seeds of their personal narratives and see in them the potential for other modes. "My Trip to Ecuador" can be extended and shaped until readers recognize it as travel writing. "My Thirty-Six Dead Goldfish" can be thought of as memoirs and set alongside other published memoirs. "Why Doesn't God Make Magic Houses and Send Them Down for Homeless People" can be extended into a persuasive essay. Louis began with a piece called "Today the Cockroaches Came Back" but then decided to turn his personal narrative into a report.

LOUIS (*reading*): "A cockroach is an insect. Cockroaches are very fast runners. It is very hard to catch them. They run and hide very fast. Cockroaches' enemies are people. Cockroaches are house pests. Cockroaches eat little crumbs on the floor. They live in water pipes and under stoves. Every time people try to catch them they run to where they live, but sometimes the people catch them. . . . Once when I was lying down on the sofa . . ."

LUCY CALKINS: Often as children reread their writing they hear patterns and rhythm, see images, and decide to rework their pieces into poems.

RACHEL (*reading*): Father, I wish you didn't have to go to work.
I wish you could stay at home.
I wish you could stay at home and play with me all day long.
I wish you'd have more time for play.

LUCY CALKINS: Writing, then, has many purposes. Jeter uses writing to thank a visiting author:

JETER (*reading*): "Dear Elizabeth Levy: I would like to thank you for having us over to your house and for coming to our classroom. Your advice on my story was wonderful and really helped. My story sounds much better as a poem. Thank you for having us over at your house. I was really amazed to see that an author's house would be that big. I had a different idea about your house. I thought it would be small and crammed with file cabinets. Thank you again. Sincerely, Jeter."

LUCY CALKINS: But of course, in the beginning there's the blank page, and for many of our youngsters that blank page is a challenge. They come to us asking, "What should I write about?" We try to help them realize that writers generally choose their own topics, and that good topics don't materialize out of thin air. When people write regularly, when they get into their stride as writers, they live with the consciousness of "I am one who writes," and they find potential topics everywhere, just as poet Georgia Heard does.

GEORGIA HEARD: Most of my ideas come from different places. Sometimes I kind of keep a journal and I put a piece of paper in the typewriter and I have the date and I just free write, and a lot of my ideas come from that. Other times I'm walking on the street and something occurs to me, or I see something, and I'm moved by it and I come and write about that. Other times, usually I have a poem going, a whole pile of poems going, and I come home and I read them, and ideas stem from the work that I'm already doing. Other times I pick up a book and I read and I get ideas from that . . . various places.

LUCY CALKINS: Children, too, develop a repertoire of strategies for finding important things to write about. Very young children, we find, rarely plan their stories prior to writing them. Instead they're apt to just pick up a marker pen and begin to draw. When they're given the opportunity to talk about those drawings, stories often emerge from them, as in this conference with Martha Horn.

MARTHA: How about this part right here? I see something . . .

JOHN: That's the fire from the volcano.

MARTHA: Oh . . . so here's this volcano and there's a fire coming out of it . . . and what's happening?

JOHN: The house is blowing up . . .

MARTHA: The fire is coming down onto the house and the house is blowing up?

JOHN: No. Blowing up.

MARTHA: Blowing up? From the fire?

JOHN: Yup.

MARTHA: Ohh! Is anyone in the house?

JOHN: Nope.

MARTHA: No. Good thing.

JOHN: They ran out. That's why, there was a big fire.

MARTHA: They ran out because of the big fire. And there's all kinds of things happening over here. [*Looks at the picture.*] How about this part over here? This is real interesting.

JOHN: That's a butterfly.

MARTHA: So there's this volcano erupting, and all this fire coming down onto the house, and the house blows up, and there's this giant butterfly right here?

JOHN: Yeah, it is. And it's big.

MARTHA: And it's big.

JOHN: And it's nice. So it flew and taked the people out of the house.

MARTHA: Ohh, the butterfly is going to take all the people?

JOHN: No. Take them out of the house.

MARTHA: . . . out of the house, so they wouldn't get burned?

JOHN: Yup.

MARTHA: John, if you were going to write something about this story— you just told me all that stuff—if you were going to write one thing, one very important thing about your story, what do you think you might want to write?

JOHN: I wrote words over here [*turns drawing over to show letters*].

MARTHA: Oh . . . you did . . . can you read them to me? Here's a story, and here's all the words?

JOHN: You know what that says?

MARTHA: No. I want you to read it to me.

JOHN: It says, "The zebra was trying to eat all the food."

LUCY CALKINS: It helps students to know what their friends are writing about, because good topics, we find, are contagious. Sometimes a child who is stuck can be encouraged to move around the classroom as a researcher might, noticing, even documenting, what others are writing about.

Children often get ideas from each other. Maria's piece is about throwing birdseed in her hair and pretending it was a veil and this was her wedding day. This sparks the idea in Roberto that he, too, might write about pretending. His next story will be about how, when he feeds the pigeons on his roof, he makes believe they are messenger pigeons carrying coded secrets to spies.

Sometimes when children feel they have nothing to write about they look over their past pieces of writing, returning to topics they've written on earlier. We need to teach children that this is okay, that good topics are not used up. So often they'll say to us, "I can't write about my brother, I already wrote about *him*," not realizing that we all have only a few seminal issues in our lives, and that these are like quarries from which we can mine a huge variety of pieces.

Then, too, writers find real reasons to write when they attach writing to the projects and purposes of their lives. These kindergarteners have kept records of their chicks' growth.

A CHILD: We love you, Tuffy . . . and we love you, chick.

LUCY CALKINS: This writer [Vinnie] is observing the class mascot [the guinea pig] so that he can weave true bits of information into his fiction story. He learned the role research plays even in fiction writing when he learned that Robert McCloskey kept ducks in his bathtub while he worked on *Make Way for Ducklings*.

Then, too, some young writers, like the poet Georgia Heard, find inspiration in the books they read and the things they see around them.

RICHARD: The way I got the idea of stallions and the motorcycle is because when I finished reading this book called *Thunder, the Mighty Stallion of the Hill* . . . so I looked out the window one day, and I saw a black motorcycle riding down the street, so I said, "Why can't I compare a motorcycle to a stallion," because stallions do lots of things that motorcycles do, except they don't have wheels. 'Cause stallions don't have wheels, they just have four legs. So . . . 'cause I wrote in this part, it's over here . . . "their hooves thundering, kicking up dust like black motorcycles riding, riding in the dirt," 'cause when a black stallion keeps on running in the dirt he kicks up dirt behind him, and when a black motorcycle does skids with his back wheel, all the smoke comes up.

LUCY CALKINS: A teacher's first role, then, is to help youngsters tap into real reasons to write. Then, too, by establishing workshops which are structured in simple predictable ways we can provide young people with what they need to become strategic, planful writers. The predictable structure, the predictable schedule, layout, and expectations, are important. When students know, for example, they'll be writing the first thing every afternoon for an hour, they anticipate that writing time. As Don Graves says, "They write when they're not writing."

HILARY: When I'm in bed . . . and I usually get the pictures before thinking, not when I'm sleeping, but before when I'm thinking. So what I do . . . I'm thinking—and I can't make too much noise because my sister's in the room, sleeping—so what I do is, I have tissues next to my bed and I have a desk right near it too and I take a pencil and write on the tissue, and then in the morning, I rethink my dream totally, like everything . . . what happened, so I can write it.

LUCY CALKINS: Like Hilary, many professional writers value having a predictable time and place for writing. They also value their tools.

GEORGIA HEARD: It's very important that I work in this room. I have all of my books here, all of my favorites, and I can just stand up and pick them and read from them. Also, it's a very familiar environment. I live here. It's always the same light, I always have the same picture out the window, my papers in the same spot, all my poems are in this drawer . . . it's very comfortable. I feel very safe here.

LUCY CALKINS: I can't stress enough the importance of tools. Rather than just telling children that a run-on draft can be cut into several stories, we provide them with scissors and tape. The tools embody a philosophy. Scissors, staplers, and Scotch tape help students view early drafts as tentative. They help students approach writing as more like playing in clay than inscribing in marble. File boxes filled with cumulative folders encourage students to save and honor their messy drafts, and to look back on them as records of their growth and as seedbeds for future pieces of writing. Lucite frames and photo albums convey so much about the way we view students' writing.

But the most important writing tool of all may be wonderful literature. As Robert Cormier says, "I learn to write by reading. Reading's the most important thing I do besides the actual writing." Children learn by reading famous authors, by reading each other. Yesterday a child told me, "I have three favorite authors: E. B. White, Katherine Paterson, and Randalio." We can help children not only love literature but also learn from it. Here, JoAnn Curtis has gathered a group of children together, and she is pointing out a specific lesson they can learn from their reading.

JOANN CURTIS: You know, in a good mystery there is not only a mystery for the writer but there's a mystery for the reader. A good mystery has the reader discovering what the mystery is, and the reader is also involved in trying to solve the mystery. When I took your writing folders home over the weekend, many of you, in your mysteries, you told me in the very first page of your mystery what the mystery was. So by the time I was reading through the mysteries, it wasn't like I was helping you to solve them because I knew all along what problem, what the mystery was all about. And so I thought what would be helpful for some of you today, before you start working on your writing, is for us to pull together over at the round table—those of you who are working on mysteries—and to talk about the books that we've been reading. I know many of you have been reading mystery stories too. And I thought maybe we could spend some time talking about the ways the writers in your books are going about getting the reader involved. Okay, so let's do that. Those of you working on mysteries, meet at the round table and the rest of you can get started on your writing.

LUCY CALKINS: Scotch tape and scissors are important, files and photo albums are important, literature is important, but above all writers of all ages value having colleagues who can help them with their writing.

[Scene in which a cluster of children help one child spell the word morning.*]*

LUCY CALKINS: I know for myself that although writing is an individual enterprise, I need to bracket the time alone with times when I have professional company, people to listen and to extend, people to cheer me on and to help. Children can provide this sort of professional company for each other.

ROBERT (*reading his writing*): "Time passed as wave after wave of smoke passed over the blazing flames. Finally I could hear sirens in the distance. The firemen were finally coming! In only a few seconds the firemen were spraying the building with water. It would be several hours before the fire would be over. Now . . ."

PAUL: Is it a nuclear bomb or just . . . ?

ROBERT: No it's not, it's a fire.

SCOTT: No, it's real. It actually happened to him.

ROBERT: No, this is real, this is real. What happens is that someone, it was an arsonist-type guy. He had a torch and a thing of oil and it blew up, and that's how come it was like a mushroom cloud.

PAUL: Remember what we were saying . . . because I thought it was like World War III.

ROBERT: Well . . . I guess it *does* seem like that.

PAUL: The building helps it, because before you just said a mushroom cloud rose up in the air, and it sounded like, you know, wow, the fire was going and on the other side, a side show, World War III.

ROBERT: Well, let me see . . . I wrote, "Boom, a mushroom cloud rose from the building."

PAUL: Good, yeah, that's good . . .

ROBERT: Yes but, you see, when I say, "For a moment I thought that the building was being bombed," it tells you that it *wasn't* being bombed.

PAUL: I think it's confusing . . .

ROBERT: Yeah, okay, well, I could change it . . .

LUCY CALKINS: In each of these instances, the way children help each other says a lot about the kinds of response models their teachers have provided. Back when I went to school the only response I received to my writing were marginal "awks" and "run-ons." Writing for me was, as Mina Shaughnessey says, "but a line which creeps across the page, exposing as it goes all that the writer does not know." Writing put me on the line and I didn't want to be there. Back then, if we'd been asked to help each other, we would have zealously marked up each other's errors.

Children listen and respond authentically to each other, asking writer's questions, if their teachers are doing this in one-to-one writing conferences.

"But I have thirty-two students," teachers say to me, "How can I have one-to-one conferences?" My best response is to bring teachers into crowded New York City classrooms, to invite them to watch teachers like JoAnn as she moves about the classroom. Or I ask teachers to pull in close to watch teachers like Martha, who are acting as a coach —listening, understanding, celebrating, and extending what the student has done.

[Scenes in which Martha Horn helps Schallon spell macaroni *and post the shopping list on the refrigerator.]*

LUCY CALKINS: Here again, Martha understands and then celebrates.

MARTHA: Shuh-Hung, you know what I was noticing? The other day you did this story about the trains, and yesterday you wrote this story about trains, and now today you have a story about tracks. It looks like *all* these stories are about trains and tracks . . .

SHUH-HUNG: Yeah.

MARTHA: Can you tell me, why you're so . . . writing so much about trains?

SHUH-HUNG: It's a teaching story.

MARTHA: It's a teaching story? What do you mean by that?

SHUH-HUNG: They know what means trains.

MARTHA: Who will know?

SHUH-HUNG: If someones don't know about trains, then the teaching book will teach them.

LUCY CALKINS: It is also helpful in conferences to expand a student's repertoire of writing strategies. For example, many students spend very little time thinking about, researching, and developing their topics before or during writing. In this conference, Shelley Harwayne emphasizes a strategy which can help not only with this piece but with many future pieces.

ALEX (*reading his writing*): "When you're a teenager you need ten hours; when you're a grown-up you need eight to nine hours of sleep. There are four stages of sleep. The first stage is when you are drowsy and in a light sleep. The next stage is REM, rapid eye movements. This is when you have your dreams. The third stage is when . . ."

SHELLEY: Oh, that's the part you're up to now? You're going to go to the third stage? So, you're thinking this is kind of boring now? [*Alex nods.*] You know, one thing I learned from E. B. White (you know E. B. White's work?) when I've been reading about him, I heard that throughout the whole writing of *Charlotte's Web*, he kept this little spider in a matchbox, and he kept it propped up right in front of him as he was writing. He studied that spider and tried to learn everything about spiders from really watching and watching. Certainly his book isn't boring. Maybe Alex, you can be doing what E. B. White does. He could be your writing teacher. Maybe what you need to do is really watch people when they are sleeping and talk to people about their sleeping habits. Become a little bit of a reporter. Maybe take a little pad and put it in your jean pocket, and when you go home tonight you could be talking to your sister or your parents or relatives who come to the house and *really* try to learn about sleep. My guess is if you just fill up that notebook, that you'll just come to class with rich ideas for making your piece *so* interesting. Why don't you have a go at it?

LUCY CALKINS: John Ciardi said that a writer is both passion hot and critic cold, that writing involves a tension between creation and criticism. But often in our classrooms, our kids are passion hot and we are critic cold. Both functions belong in the writer. In conferences, we can help children to reread and to assess their own writing.

JOANN CURTIS: Farah, I know that you've just finished this piece?

FARAH: Yeah.

JOANN: This was a favorite?

FARAH: This is one of my favorites.

JOANN: This is one of your favorite ones. Could you read me just a little bit of the beginning?

FARAH (*reading*): One day my mother had a baby and I loved it. It was a boy and its eyes were blue and it had yellow hair and he was a cute baby. His name was John. He liked to play with me.

JOANN: I can see why it is one of your favorites. You know, when you write something really well, it's important that you take a moment to study it. Look and see what it was that you did. I think maybe before you start another piece of writing, what would be nice for you to do, Farah, is to take your finished folder and open it up and read through all your pieces, and sort of put them in order. Put the ones that you think are the best on the top and kind of rank them like that. I'm going to go away and let you work on it. I'll come back in a little while and we can talk about what you've found, okay?

LUCY CALKINS: Often in conferences we help students use their reading books as resources.

JOANN CURTIS: And there are going to be different chapters in your book? [*turns to published books*]. Sort of like . . . let's see, one of these was like that, wasn't it? The one on *Let's Be Indians*. It had different chapters . . . Did you look at this Table of Contents to see how they organized this book?

ANDREW: No.

JOANN: It might be helpful for you to do that, because this is sort of a book about how to make things, too . . . And if you look at the chapters, it's like headbands, "How to Make a Headband," "How to Make an Indian Costume."

ANDREW: A headband's easy . . . go find a pigeon feather.

JOANN: You know what you might want to do before you go back and get started working on your book is you might want to look . . . open up to the chapter that says headbands and see what this author did to organize it. How did he go about writing the chapter on headbands? That might give you some ideas for when you go back to do your book on how to make things. Okay? I'm going to leave you . . . and let you look through this . . .

SHELLEY HARWAYNE: You've got this big sheet right here in front of you. Well, maybe I could help you for just a bit. We could chat. I've been reading about this incredible writer, Kathryn Lasky. Have you ever heard of her? She's just a *fine* writer, and I hope you'll get to read some of her work one day. And she has this way of coming up with topics that's just so special and it might help you. She says that when she wants to figure out what she's going to write about, she thinks so hard about all the things that are so curious to her, things she *really* wonders about and tries to understand. She has this book called *Sugaring Time*, and it's all about how they get maple sugar and maple syrup from those trees. Even as a little kid she just wondered how it happened. So she went off to investigate and that became a whole book on sugaring. And then she's got this other book that came out last year that's super, and it's all how marionettes work. It's called *Puppeteer*. She said she always wondered how they pulled those strings and stuff. So she set off to learn about that. Maybe what you can do is just what Kathryn Lasky does. Sit here for a minute and use this sheet to make a list of some of the things you've always wondered about and you've never quite taken the time to understand them. They could very well turn out to be topics for you. Could you try that?

MARY: Yes.

SHELLEY: And, Mary, if it doesn't work, you come see me and we'll come up with something else.

MARY: Okay.

LUCY CALKINS: One of the most important things to remember is that our conferences don't always turn out. We can back up and approach them from another direction, but in the end we need to know how to make a graceful exit.

JOANN CURTIS: You know, I learned a lot about you. I learned about Nick being a good friend, I learned about . . .

SALVATORE (*correcting her*): Nicky. . . . Oh, I forgot to put the *y* on.

JOANN: I learned about that. I learned about how you have these dogs at home and you really like the dogs. And you were talking about cat and dog fights. I learned about your mother and your father and your VHS, and I learned about how you like to play video games. I'm wondering, with all the different things that you mentioned in here, is there one of them that is more important to you than some of the others?

SALVATORE: No, well, I didn't mention a lot of things. I skipped . . . I want

to make . . . I want to make . . . see, I just put "About Me—Part One."
I can make two, three . . . see, in one, why did I put that? Because if
it becomes good, then I could write number two and so on.

JOANN: I see . . .

SALVATORE: If it becomes good, I'll make all of them.

JOANN: So this story started out as trying to be All About You.

SALVATORE: Yeah.

JOANN: One of my suggestions for you as a writer is that I think it would
be a bit of a challenge and a good thing for you if you could look in
the story and see if you could choose just *one* of these ideas that you
have a lot to say about. Could you take a minute and just look it over?
See if you could find one of those ideas that . . .

SALVATORE: What?

JOANN: That . . . that you like a lot or that you have a lot to say about.

SALVATORE: I already know. I like *all* of them. I like the video games, I like
my VHS, I like my dogs . . .

JOANN: If you were to choose one of these ideas that you could help grow
into a story all of its own, which idea would it be?

SALVATORE: What do you mean, what idea?

JOANN: Well, you said you liked video games, you liked the part about
the dog and the cats, you liked the part about your parents. If you were
to choose *one* of these ideas . . .

SALVATORE: But this is, um . . . a good story, you know. I liked the other
ones that I made, but I don't know where the other story that I made,
I don't know where that is.

JOANN: I see. Okay, well, thanks for sharing this with me.

SALVATORE: Bye.

LUCY CALKINS: In *The Art of Teaching Writing*, I suggest that our job as
writing teachers is to put ourselves out of a job. We need to confer with
our students in part in order to demonstrate ways children can confer
with each other. Students can become very helpful writing coaches for
each other.

LESLIE: [*Reading her writing*] It was around 1 A.M. The clock on the mantel
chimed once and died down. Henny got up and walked into the living
room, plopping herself on the couch. While she watched the sparks of
fire rise up through the chimney, she made herself comfortable and
thought about all her bad dreams.

SUZANNE: Well, I know what you mean about you want to keep all the
description. Maybe you could have her doing the actions, and making
her really plopping herself on the couch and everything really happening.

LESLIE: Yeah, but how would I write that down on paper?

SUZANNE: You could have stage directions and you could have her . . .

LESLIE: What do you mean?

SUZANNE: . . . write in parentheses saying "(Henny gets up)" . . .

LESLIE: Oh, yeah, yeah, I see . . .

SUZANNE: So then everybody will get into the mood and know what's going on.

LESLIE: That's a good idea.

LUCY CALKINS: All of the teaching in a writing workshop is not contained within the parameters of small conferences. Often children gather together at the end of a writing workshop to assist a single writer. Of course, sometimes writers bring finished work to these share meetings, and they become a time for celebration.

RICHARD (*reading his poem*):

Stallions.
Stallions are black.
Black like the night.
When you see them,
they look like black motorcycles
riding in the night
Their hooves thundering, kicking up dust,
like black motorcycles
riding, riding in the dirt,
their long manes flying in the wind,
their long tails whipping back and forth
like black motorcycles doing skids in the street.

[*Everyone claps.*]

JOANN CURTIS: I want to ask you to try something new. Would you just turn to somebody sitting next to you and very quietly, would you whisper to them what it was that you liked about Richard's poem, what kinds of questions or comments you want to make to him. We'll just do that for a minute first. [Pause.] Are you guys ready to tell Richard what you think about his writing? Okay, turn around. Let's look at Richard. Raise your hand if you have something to say.

ERIC: I like the way you're comparing a stallion and a motorcycle, like when you say that when the stallion runs it kicks up dust and makes a cloud of smoke and when the motorcycle rides in dust and dirt that that makes a cloud of smoke too.

JOANN: Another way that we can talk to Richard about his piece is by asking questions about how he went about writing it. Now that the piece is all finished, we could ask him about where the idea came from, how he went about writing his piece. Why don't we try that? Does anyone have a question that they'd like to ask Richard about the way . . . ?

PAT: Why did you make the story like a poem, into a poem?

RICHARD: 'Cause I like to write poems and I like the way they sound, 'cause I like rhymes. I like the way I write them 'cause I think my readers will enjoy them and *I* enjoy them.

JOANN: You know, many of you are writing poetry. Some of you may like to pull Richard aside during writing time and talk a little bit further about his poem and maybe the work, what you've learned from writing your poem is something you could share with some of the other writers. Thanks for sharing your writing with us, Richard.

LUCY CALKINS: Reading your own work aloud to a whole group of friends is exciting and scary, as Moira tells us.

MOIRA: I felt, um, a little bit nervous.

SHELLEY HARWAYNE: You were a little nervous?

MOIRA: Yeah, but I speaked up.

SHELLEY: You did. What were you thinking?

MOIRA: I was thinking if the kids would say, "Boo!"

LUCY CALKINS: I've known the fear Moira talks about, and the sense that when I share my writing I'm uncovering and sharing who I am. That's the power of writing. It invites us to put ourselves on the line, to bring ourselves into classrooms, into the teaching-learning transaction. And that has made a world of difference.

ERICA (*reading*): "Life and Death: My great-grandfather died. I think he was 85 or 88 years old. I went to the funeral when he died. I was only two years old. I was ashamed because I was afraid of him. I was afraid because I never spent time with him so I couldn't know how kind he was. I loved him so much but I didn't have the courage to tell him. I always spent time with my great-grandmother. I love my family, my whole entire family. Let me tell you something. Never lose your courage to tell someone you love them because if you do you're making the same mistake I did. I love you, Great-Grandfather, I really love you."

JILL: That gave me a feeling, like, when my great-grandmother died, and I only saw her a few times too, and I have the same feeling like you. I never told her I loved her, like you never told your grandfather? And I feel the same way.

DENISE: What made you pick that story? What made you feel that you had to pick that story?

ERICA: I wanted to get the words out of me but I just didn't—kept them inside of me, and so I thought I'd share this story so everybody could know . . . how it would be like and how I feel.

CHRISTIAN: I never really used to be . . . I never really talked to my grandmother because she only speaks Italian. She can't talk anything else, and when I try to talk to her and she says, "Huh? Huh?" And then you try to talk to her and you only have to talk to her in Italian or else she don't understand you.

BETH: Why were you scared?

ERICA: I was scared 'cause, it's like, you know when you see a stranger, and you don't know him so well and you say "Hi" and that's it. Or if you don't say nothing at all or just like if I, all I said was "Hi" and I didn't say "I love you."

10

Workshop Materials

A

Viewers' Sheet

This form may be used with a first or only viewing of the videotape, as suggested in chapter 3.

Viewers may want to record their responses to the videotape alongside the specific episode. The counter should be set at zero when the phrase "Dedicated to the teachers and children of New York City" leaves the screen.

Episode	Counter Reading	Responses
Calkins is suggesting that the writing workshop provides a new image of what classrooms can sound, feel, and look like.	0025–0073	
Calkins is talking about real reasons to write.	0074–0098	
Richard is talking about how he writes to get out the madness.	0099–0108	
David explains where his ideas for writing come from.	0109–0116	
Calkins is talking about personal narratives as seedbeds for other modes.	0117–0134	

Episode	Counter Reading	Responses
Louis is reading his report on cockroaches.	0135–0149	
Marisol is reading her poem "Father."	0149–0160	
Jeter is reading his thank-you letter.	0161–0177	
Calkins discusses good topics.	0178–0191	
Georgia Heard tells where her topics come from.	0192–0212	
Calkins is talking about young children's topic choice.	0213–0223	
Martha Horn is conferring with a kindergarten child about his volcano drawing.	0224–0278	
Calkins is talking about classroom strategies for finding a topic.	0279–0309	
Kindergarten children are keeping a record of their chicks' growth.	0310–0316	
Vinnie is studying the guinea pig.	0317–0324	
Richard is explaining how he was inspired by a book he read.	0325–0357	

Episode	Counter Reading	Responses
Calkins is suggesting the need for predictable workshops.	0358–0374	
Hilary is explaining when her best topics came to her.	0375–0391	
Heard describes the importance of her writer's tools.	0392–0409	
Calkins is talking about the importance of students' writing tools, including literature.	0410–0444	
JoAnn Curtis is suggesting children learn from the mysteries they are reading.	0445–0473	
Young children are helping a five-year-old spell *morning*.	0474–0502	
Older students are helping a peer clarify his meaning.	0503–0548	
Calkins is talking about teachers who model one-to-one writing conferences.	0549–0577	
Martha Horn is helping a young child spell *macaroni*.	0578–0630	

Episode	Counter Reading	Responses
Martha Horn is talking to a five-year-old about his teaching books.	0631–0652	
Shelley Harwayne is offering a research strategy to Alex, who is working on a report about sleep.	0653–0700	
Calkins is talking about encouraging students to be critical readers.	0701–0709	
Curtis is encouraging Farah to evaluate and rank her finished work.	0710–0733	
Curtis is suggesting that Andrew study the "how-to" books in the class library.	0734–0766	
Harwayne is suggesting that Mary try Kathryn Lasky's strategy for finding an important topic.	0767–0801	
Curtis is struggling to help Salvatore focus his writing.	0802–0856	
An older student is helping a friend turn her draft into play form.	0857–0888	
Richard is reading his poem at a share meeting.	0889–0908	

Episode	Counter Reading	Responses
Curtis is suggesting new ways to respond to the writer.	0909–0956	
Moira shares her fears about reading aloud.	0957–0964	
Calkins is talking about the power of writing.	0965–0974	
Erica shares her piece about her great-grandfather.	0975–1036	

B

Two-Column Log

This chart may be used with a first or only viewing of the videotape, as suggested in chapter 3. It provides a way for participants to synthesize their learning.

What I Am Learning	*What I Need to Know*

C

Dilemmas Surrounding Topic Choice

These problematic situations can be used in the activity "Anticipate and Address Concerns over Topic Choice," as suggested in the "Strategies for Finding Topics" section of chapter 4. They may be considered in small or large groups. Each is discussed in Workshop Materials D.

1   Mrs. Jones decides to give the idea of topic choice a chance in her classroom. She gathers students together and tells them, "Today you can all choose your own topics for writing."

"Do we have to choose our own topics?" students ask. There are worried lines on their foreheads. "Give us some ideas," they plead.

Mrs. Jones knows that if she provides several possible topics, her students remain dependent on her. She wants, instead, to provide her students with strategies that will help them find their own topics. What are some strategies she can suggest?

2   Twenty minutes into the writing workshop, Mrs. Jones sees that four of her students are still sitting with blank pages in front of them. What should she do?

3   Mrs. Mitchell's fourth graders are studying the history of their town. For many years, students immersed in this social studies unit have written books entitled "My Town." Mrs. Mitchell is concerned that the new emphasis on topic choice will mean that she can no longer link social studies and writing. Is she right?

4   Youngsters in Mr. Wadsworth's class have been choosing their own topics for several months. Topic choice seems almost effortless for them. Yet Mr. Wadsworth is not pleased with the topics his youngsters choose. Several are writing about smelly farts, others seem to get great pleasure

in detailed descriptions of the nasty food in their school cafeteria. Others choose broad topics like friends, school, and family.

Mr. Wadsworth dutifully tries to stay out of his students' way and to give them full rein over their topics. But underneath, he questions whether this is the best thing to do and rails against a program that idealizes freedom at the cost of rigor.

D

Discussion of Dilemmas Surrounding Topic Choice

The following comments relate to the situations presented in Workshop Materials C.

1 It is important that the writing strategies we share with our students are not gimmicky "prewriting" activities but instead, methods writers might naturally use. It is also important for teachers and youngsters to realize that any one writer will feel more at home with some strategies than with others. There is no reason for the entire class to use the same set of strategies.

Course instructors can draw possible strategies from these references:

- Murray, Donald. *Write to Learn*. New York: Holt, Rinehart & Winston, 1984. Chapters 2 and 3.
- Elbow, Peter. *Writing with Power*. New York: Oxford University Press, 1981. Chapters 2, 7, 8.
- Graves, Donald. *Writing: Teachers & Children at Work*. Portsmouth, NH: Heinemann, 1983. Pp. 179–82.

The most important source for writing strategies, however, will always be reflections on our own writing processes. Instructors will probably want to suggest these strategies to teachers working with young writers:

- Some writers keep a list of possible topics for writing on the inside cover of their daily writing folder.
- Some writers jot ideas, events, scenes, and feelings that interest them into their logs or daybooks. Murray likens these collections to a compost pile; when ideas are thrown together in this fashion, they ferment, and new things begin to grow.

- Free writing, brainstorming, and making lists can help some writers.
- Good ideas are contagious. Writers will learn from the work of their friends, their teacher, the authors they read.
- Sometimes it helps to choose a genre first and then the topic. For example, a writer may begin by deciding to write a song, a recipe, a play, a diary . . . and topics will flow from that choice.
- Writers can find new topics from the discarded material that accumulated in writing earlier pieces.
- Writers can decide to return to an old topic.

2 Instructors will find Calkins's response to this situation in her book *The Art of Teaching Writing*, pp. 123–26, 175–82.

3 First of all, Mrs. Mitchell needs reassurance. Of all the important ideas in current theories on teaching writing, none is more important than the notion that teachers are professionals, who must draw on all that they know and believe in order to create wise ways of teaching. Mrs. Mitchell is a professional and as such, she must decide what happens in her curriculum.

   The videotape and current books on teaching writing suggest teaching practices but leave decisions in the hands of teachers.

   Of course, in this instance there is no contradiction between Mrs. Mitchell's ideas and those espoused in the videotape. Children need not choose their topics *all* the time, and they can certainly choose topics that fall under an umbrella idea such as "My Town."

4 Mr. Wadsworth is probably representative of many teachers who feel that adopting new ideas on teaching writing means that instead of following one's instincts, one follows a prescribed course. What a shame it is that he isn't trusting his instincts! *Of course* these students need their teacher to question—and, if necessary, to outlaw—their silly stories on farts. *Of course* these youngsters would benefit from their teacher's advice on good topics.

Dwayne's Writing Folder

This collection of pieces can be used as suggested in chapter 6. It represents a first grader's growth in writing over the course of one year. Comments about each of the pieces are included after the samples of writing. It might be helpful to inform teachers that these pieces are not the only writing Dwayne did during this eight-month period. Instead, they were selected by his teacher as representative of his development during first grade.

September—Castle Drawing

September—Children with Cat

October—Truck Drawing—"BABY" Label

October—Fruit Poster

Early November

Dwayne

one go out they
house we go out
we work city.

Late November

the Spet ws

fre a BABy

None B t toBABy
ouB t toBABy
the BABy Eddy

December—Page 1

by Dwayne

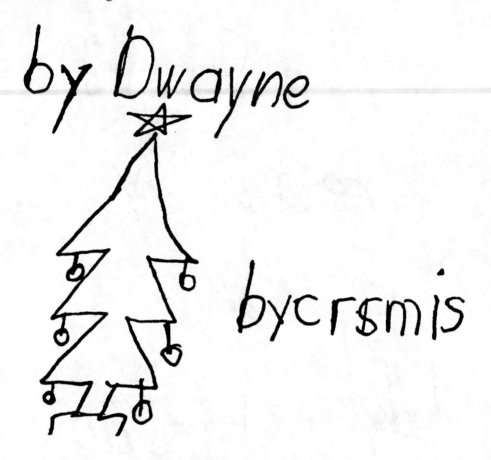

bycrsmis

December—Page 2

thecrrsmis
tRe

December—Page 3

December—Page 4

satcloiscme

January

One day a spidere was hangereae. Then a grasshoper was stake in the spider's webe. And then the spider sewk the grassh blod. Then any more was the spider hangereae.
The End of the store

February—Title Page

Fishis

by

Dwayne Tejada

P.S.173 Publishing Company

February—Page 2

To Eddy, my best friend

February—Page 3

The little fish wanted something to eat. The fish saw a snoker She woted to eat it. The little fish eat it. Then a big fish wated something to eat. Then the big fish eat the little fish. And the bigise one woted something to eat too. And then the bigise eat all the fish.

February—Page 4

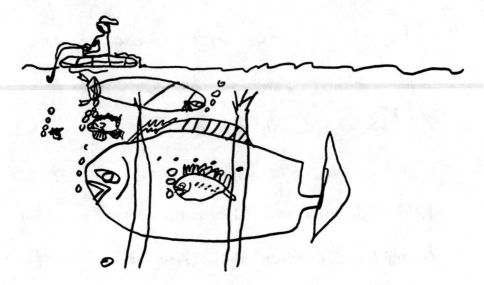

February—Page 5

Then a fisher came to get a fish. The fisher was fishing. Then The bigise got to the string. Then the fish fisher and her famuly ate the big fish.

March—Cartoon

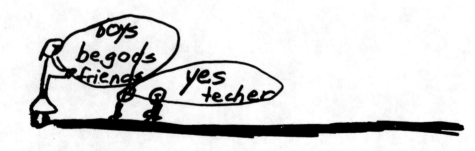

March—Script for Puppets

Dwayne

Cow: Mo Mo hay you want
to go for a walk

Sheep: Ma Ma chor let's go

Cow: Will you takthis fly out
of my tail

Sheep: Chor. get on me
and let's go

The following information accompanies each piece of Dwayne's writing. Participating teachers can discern some of it from closely examining each sample of writing. But some of the information is based on background knowledge, and therefore participating teachers cannot be expected to find it from the sample of writing alone.

- September—Castle drawing.

  Dwayne's drawing is rich in detail. After he drew this picture he told a story of a prince and princess who live in a beautiful castle. He made no attempt to write words. There is a possibility that the boat has a boxed-in backward *B* on it.

- September—Children with cat.

  Dwayne's drawing has decreased in size and detail. When asked about the drawing, he told the story of a cat that follows a boy and girl to school. The boxed-in B appears again. Dwayne has made no attempt to encode the story in print. Instead it seems that he has put down random letters because he has realized that people use letters when they write.

- October—Truck drawing—"Baby" label

  Dwayne told the story of driving a truck in New York City traffic. There was no baby in the story, but the word had become a sight word for him, and in October he began putting it on most of his pieces. It's also interesting that Dwayne has begun to write his name as an author might: "by Dwayne." He has become very conscious of the other writers in the class.

- October—Fruit poster

  For a while, in October, Dwayne began copying words off signs and posters in the class. When asked to read this particular piece of writing he said, "It tells you about good food." He views this piece of his writing as a poster for his classroom's nutrition center.

- Early November—House drawing and label

  Again in early November, Dwayne relied on the texts around him. Here he has copied words from a small reader he found in the class library. It's significant to notice that Dwayne pays less attention to his drawing when he writes words, even when the words are not his own.

- Late November—"Baby Eddy" piece

  In late November, Dwayne returned to writing his own texts, combining a few sight words with random strings. His text has begun to look more like a sentence. It even begins with "the." *Baby* seems to be a safe word for Dwayne, and he has also used his best friend's name, Eddy. When asked to read his story, Dwayne now tells one that matches the context of the picture, although it still does not seem coordinated in length with the "words" he has written. In reading the piece, he tells about a baby named Eddy who liked to play in the park.

- December—Christmas book

This Christmas story marked a big breakthrough for Dwayne. He has now begun to use precise words to say what he means, and his invented spellings are close approximations. It is also the first time he has written a book with several pages.

Page 1 reads: by Dwayne
by Christmas [indicating he is still on new ground with the word *by*].

Page 2:   the Christmas tree [a label for his picture].

Page 3:   The Christmas party [a label for his picture].

Page 4:   Santa Claus is coming [Again, his drawings have taken a back seat to his writing. He now begins to write a story.]

- January—Hungry spider story

Dwayne's January text indicates that he no longer prefers to draw before he writes. He has begun to select wide-lined paper. It is clear that Dwayne is now comfortable spelling new words and that his visual memory of words is increasing. The text reads: "One day a spider was hungry. Then a grasshopper was stuck in the spider's web. And then the spider suck the grasshopper's blood. Then any more was the spider hungry. The end of the story."

- February—Fishes

Dwayne's book about fish demonstrates some of the reading-writing connections he's making. He now has a title page, complete with the author's full name and the publishing company. His second page is the dedication, and now "Eddy" is used appropriately. Dwayne's spellings are very complete, and he has begun to use his drawings to illustrate the text, not to rehearse for it.

- March—Cartoon and animal dialogue

  The last two pieces in Dwayne's folder indicate that he has begun to write in a variety of modes. He made the cartoon after the class read cartoons in a children's news weekly. After his teacher added paper and pencils to the pretend area in March, he wrote a script for the animal finger puppets.

F

The Spelling Strategies of Our Young Writers

The following form, with its examples of young children's writing, may be used in connection with the activity "Study and Observe Children's Spelling Strategies" in chapter 6.

Samples of Young Children's Writing *Spelling Strategies*

1.

   Loxe is Jam bode ve Ciss
   Then tucy mak love Then they
   Srt Ciss On then maowf.
   Wet they are in a cra they srt
   to ciss mrow ciss and ciss and ciss.

   Love is somebody you kiss
   Then they make love then they
   start kissing on their mouth.
   When they are in a car they start
   to kiss more kiss and kiss and kiss.

Samples of Young Children's Writing   *Spelling Strategies*

2.

WE R LRNG
TO RED
SAM BACSREJ
BAT SAM BACSR
HOD

We are learning
to read
Some books are easy
but some books are
hard

3.

Ho ToMT
PTN BTR
1.TKOTTH
BD
2.SDUN
+he GOePNT
BDR
3.PT UN
GrJle
4.eTT

How to make
Peanut Butter:
1.   Take out the bread.
2.   Spread on the gooey peanut butter.
3.   Put on grape jelly.
4.   Eat it.

Samples of Young Children's Writing   *Spelling Strategies*

4. I Leik THe EɑiRi
um I Leik THe
shRs

I like the aquarium.
I like the sharks.

5.

I WAT   ON
A HS

I went on
a horse.

Samples of Young Children's Writing	Spelling Strategies

6.

Lesst
Egg
Buttr
Milk
Macrone
meetBolls
escrol
SPenich
PenutButtr

List
Egg
Butter
Milk
Macaroni
Meatballs
Escarole
Spinach
Peanut Butter

G

Reflections on the Spelling Strategies of Our Young Writers

The following numbered comments relate to the writing samples in Workshop Materials F.

1   We can see from the spelling of *car* that this child is trying to remember the visual image of the word. It's obvious from the spelling "cra" that she is no longer just relying on sounding out the word. She remembers the letters in the word but can't recall their proper sequence. It seems likely that *car* will soon be added to the other words the writer knows from memory, which include *they, are, love,* and *then*.

   It's probable that "ciss" shows a reliance on phonic clues as well as a move toward using visual memory. Why else would she include the double *s*?

2   This excerpt from a letter written by a kindergarten child to his grandmother demonstrates that the child relies on the names of letters as well as on their sounds:

   • *Are* is written as *R*
   • *Easy* is written as *EZ*

3   This how-to book written by a five-year-old reads, "How to Make Peanut Butter":

   1. *Take out the bread.*
   2. *Spread on the gooey peanut butter.*
   3. *Put on grape jelly.*
   4. *Eat it.*

This young writer relies heavily on consonant sounds, mainly the initial and final sounds, but it's obvious that she also hears medial sounds, as in "PNT" (peanut) and "bDr" (butter).

4   Spelling *like* as "leik" once again indicates that the writer remembers the letters of the word but can't quite figure out their order.

5   This piece reads: "I went on a horse." The spelling of *went* as "wat" illustrates two points Susan Sowers makes in "Six Questions About Invented Spelling." She writes, "Linguists and six-year-olds know that the E in "bet" is articulated more like the letter name A than E. Say the sounds together: "-e-"-A and "-e-"-E. Feel and hear the similarity between the short E and long A."

    For the same reason, this young writer spells went "wat." Young children also omit *m*'s and *n*'s before most consonants because these are sounds not articulated. In addition, most young children would spell *jump* "jup" and *friend* "frad." In the same way, this young writer does not put an *n* in *went*.

6   This shopping list, which was hung on the toy refrigerator in the pretend kitchen, shows a combination of spelling strategies. We can guess that *milk* and *eggs* are sight words. The spelling of *butter* as "buttr" demonstrates that *l*'s and *r*'s, the liquid sounds, are often used as syllables without vowels added, because to a young child they have all the sounds they need when you say their names.

    Spinach as "spenich" and *list* as "lesst" demonstrate the same articulation strategy described in example 5. Short *i* sounds are often written as "e."

General Instructions for Creating a Character for a Role-Play

This set of suggestions may be used in connection with the activity "Role-Plays That Illustrate the Guidelines for Effective Conferences" in chapter 7.

In order to create an imaginary writer around a rough draft, workshop participants might ask questions as:

- "How does the student probably feel about the draft?"
- "What is the student planning to do next?"
- "What is the student's attitude toward writing?"
- "What kind of writing has the student already been doing?"

Once arrived at, the answers to these questions are rarely explicitly stated in the role-play but they influence the way workshop participants act in their simulated conferences. Sometimes the people who are role-playing the teacher's part in the conference do not draw this sort of information out of the writer at all, and this, of course, is something that needs to be discussed after the role-play is completed. Part of the challenge in a conference is to see if the teacher can learn about the student.

The results of creating an imaginary student writer can be illustrated. For instance, on the next page is a draft of writing written by Katherine Rose:

Summer
by Katherine Rose Glorioso
June 20, 1984

Soon it will be summer time.
We swim under wather. And
we collect crabs in the tidal pool
at sunset.
Then we sit up on the life gards chair
the chair is to high, so dad lifts
everyone up, and dad get a
herniea but mom lifetis did up
anyway

A teacher may create this character to accompany the draft:

Katherine is known as the best writer in the class. She regularly whips off short, lovely pieces. It's been a long time since she has felt that writing was a particularly challenging activity.

Migdalia, on the other hand, has written this draft:

Psat
3-4

Migdalia Pagan.
May 21, 1983

My brother
I Like my Brother because he plays
teacher with me. That's what I Like about
him. Sometimes he is bad with me, and
he's bad with my sisters. That's what I
hate about him too. That's what I get
mad about. He is bad.

Teachers may create this description of Migdalia:

Migdalia writes short pieces and quickly announces, "I'm done!" She is eager to work on her writing and would be willing to revise her work, if she knew what to do to improve her pieces. Once, when asked to make her piece better, she simply copied it over.

Teachers may create this portrait of a third student, Karen:

Each time Karen begins a piece she writes exactly two leads and then walks around the room asking her friends to note their favorite. She selects whichever one gets the most check marks and then writes the entire piece out. These are two recent leads:

<u>Leads</u>

1. It's coming up. Soon I will see my mother walking up the isle graduating from Pace University. I would be glad for two reasons. One, is because I would like to see my mother get her bachelors and two is because I would get to see her more. ✓✓✓✓✓✓✓✓

2. The day came. It was June 5, 1982. Today my mother is graduating. I am glad because now I would get to see my mother more. ✓✓

I

Donald Murray's Guidelines for Conferring

These lists may be used with the activity "Role-Plays That Illustrate the Guidelines for Effective Conferences," as explained in chapter 7.

Conference Guidelines

In responsive teaching the student acts and the teacher reacts. The range of reaction is extensive and diverse because an individual teacher is responding to an individual student, and the student in turn is passing through an ever changing process of discovery through writing. The writer follows language toward an evolving meaning, and the teacher follows the writer following language.

- *The Student Writes.*

  I cannot respond until there is at least a primitive text—lists, notes, drafts, attempts at writing.

  Any instruction I give prior to the first writing may limit or interfere with the writing my students and I do not expect to occur.

- *The Student Responds to the Text or to the Experience of Producing It.*

  The student must learn to evaluate a draft so that the student can produce a more effective draft. The teacher must know what the writer thinks of the draft to know how to read it, because the teacher's job is to help the writer make increasingly effective evaluations of the evolving draft.

Source: From Donald M. Murray, *Learning by Teaching* (Upper Montclair, NJ: Boynton/Cook Publishers, 1982), pp. 163–64. Reprinted by permission of the author.

Students know the process that produced the text. When a teacher or a fellow writer respects that process and asks the writer to articulate it, the student begins to learn the process of writing.

- *The Teacher Listens to the Student's Response to the Text and Watches How It Is Presented.*

The teacher must respect the student's potential and the student's writing experience. In the conference the student teaches the teacher the subject matter of the text and the process by which the text was produced. In teaching the teacher the students teach themselves.

How the student speaks of the draft or the writing experience may be more revealing than the text or what the student says.

- *The Teacher Reads or Listens to the Text from the Student's Perspective.*

What the student thinks of the text is the starting point for learning and teaching. The teacher will understand where the student is in the writing process if the teacher frequently experiences the process of writing, if the teacher is comfortable decoding the teacher's own evolving drafts.

- *The Teacher Responds to the Student's Response.*

The teacher attempts to give the minimal response which will help the writer produce increasingly effective drafts. The teaching is most successful when the teacher helps the student realize what the student has just learned—first the learning and then the teaching.

J

Using Stories from Authors' Lives as Resources in Conferences

This set of ideas may be used with the activity "Weave Author Anecdotes into Conferences" in the "Stories of Authors' Lives" section of chapter 8.

Sometimes after a teacher understands a particular student's writing dilemmas, the teacher will want to use an anecdote or bit of information from an author's life to help that student see how another author coped with the same dilemma. To do this, the teacher begins by listening to the student. Because students are rarely present in a staff development activity, one way to introduce teachers to the notion of bringing author anecdotes into conferences is to give teachers a synopsis of a student's writing dilemma and then to ask the teachers to either talk about or role-play ways of using what they know (or using what the instructor teaches them) about authors as they respond to that student.

For example, here is a student-portrait that the instructor might give to a group of teachers.

You are ten years old. Your writing doesn't seem to be working for you any more. You keep starting drafts and then abandoning them. They don't seem inspired or creative. You worry that you have no imagination any more. None of the tales you invent seem powerful.

In a conference with this student, a teacher might decide that the student was trying to conjure up stories out of thin air, out of imagination, and that it would help the student to hear that a familiar fiction author draws his or her ideas for a fictional story out of real-life events. The teacher could therefore tell one of the many stories provided in Workshop Materials K. The stories of Hurwitz, Hitchcock, Sendak, and L'Engle all illustrate this point.

Here is another student portrait:

You have run out of topics. In the beginning of the year, it was easy to think up new topics for writing. By now, you feel as if you have already written about every good topic. There is nothing important in your life or your mind that hasn't already been written about in a story.

In a conference, a teacher might help this student realize that, just as Monet painted his waterlilies time and again, good topics can also be written about time and again. The same characters are in many of Laura Ingalls Wilder's books, and the same is true for Louisa May Alcott's most famous books, *Little Women* and *Little Men*. The teacher might also want to point out that the student can write about the same topic in a range of genres. The teacher might illustrate this with the story about Cynthia Rylant from the author sheets in Workshop Materials K. Alternatively, the teacher could tell the student that Tomie de Paola also had difficulties coming up with topics and could suggest that the student try the strategy de Paola uses, described in the author stories in Workshop Materials K.

Instructors can create other student portraits, and teachers can find other author stories that relate to some of them. For example, if a student feels his work hasn't been appreciated by his friends, the teacher might point out that for a long time Ezra Jack Keats's artistry wasn't appreciated either. For Keats, the thing that made the difference was that he created a masterpiece *and* made sure it was very visible to the world. Perhaps that student would want to follow this example, creating a very fine and also a very public piece of writing.

If a student is reluctant to try his or her hand at fiction, the teacher might want to use L'Engle's story to illustrate one of the advantages of fiction writing.

If a student struggles over how to create a certain feeling in his or her writing, the teacher might remind the student that it helps if the writer can conjure the feeling up as he or she writes about it. The anecdote about Hitchcock might make this suggestion a more vivid one.

Of course, there will be times when the dilemma a student faces does not readily invite these sorts of author connections, and teachers need to expect this.

Stories from Authors' Lives

These stories may be used with the activity "Weave Author Anecdotes into Conferences" in the "Stories of Authors' Lives" section of chapter 8.

Tomie de Paola

When Tomie de Paola was asked if he ever worried about running out of ideas for writing, he answered, "Of course I do. . . . But I have a trick. I always try to come up with new projects before I finish the one I'm working on. . . . Sort of like sourdough bread: you take a little dough to start your new batch."

Johanna Hurwitz

In one of Johanna Hurwitz's books, a little girl goes to a fancy restaurant with her parents. She orders meatballs and spaghetti, and unfortunately one of the meatballs rolls up her sleeve. The little girl tries to inch the meatball out of her sleeve without anyone noticing.

About a week after Hurwitz's book was published, the little girl rang Hurwitz's bell and said, "Thank you for writing about me!"

"What do you mean?" asked the author.

"Oh, remember last summer when my parents had to go away and you babysat for me? When I was over here, we ate meatballs, and one rolled up my sleeve!"

When Ms. Hurwitz wrote her book, she had not realized she was drawing on something that had really happened.

Ezra Jack Keats

When Ezra Jack Keats was a little boy, his parents encouraged him to dream of being a physician. Ezra, however, had his own dreams. He wanted nothing more than to become an artist. For a long while, his parents were skeptical about their son's ambitions.

Then one day when his parents were out of the house, Ezra set to work painting the kitchen table. He did not paint it a solid white color as most people would. Instead, he used all the colors of the rainbow in order to paint rolling hills and little homes with smoke wisping out of chimneys. When he was finished, Ezra saw what he had done, and he worried over his parents' response.

When Ezra's mother came home, she gasped. "Who did this?" She added, "It is so beautiful!" When she learned it was her son's masterpiece, she covered the table with her special Friday night tablecloth. "We'll use the tablecloth for everyday use now," she said, "and remove it on Friday nights."

Robert Cormier

Robert Cormier, in talking about *The Chocolate War*, explained, "You have a rubber band that you keep pulling and pulling and pulling and just at the moment of snapping, you release it and start another chapter and start pulling again."

Alfred Hitchcock

Alfred Hitchcock reports that in order to create a sense of terror in his stories, he often recalls the terror he knew as a young boy. When Hitchcock was five years old, his father handed him a note and asked him to deliver it to a man at the police station. And so the young lad set off, the paper tucked in the pocket of his overalls. When he reached the police station, he proudly produced the note from his pocket and gave it to the man.

The man read it, and frowning down on the little boy, the man started sorting through a huge, heavy set of keys. Finding the one he wanted, the man gruffly said, "Follow me."

A moment later the little boy was being led into a dark iron cell. The little boy was locked in that pitch-dark cell for five eternally long minutes. Then he was released and sent home with the words, "That is what we do to naughty boys."

Years later, Hitchcock said, "I never forgot the sound and solidity of that clanging cell door and the bolt."

Karla Kuskin

Karla Kuskin once said that she loves words so much that she can't even throw away the fortune from a fortune cookie.

Kathryn Lasky

Kathryn Lasky explained the writing of *Puppeteer*. "I dealt with a master puppeteer, Paul Vincent Davis. I watched Paul hard at work painting the faces on the puppets he had sculpted. Suddenly Paul—a rather immense man, over two hundred fifty pounds, who certainly destroys any notions we have of little shriveled-up toymakers like Geppetto—sneezed, and ten puppets shivered and trembled. Light and dark played across their faces, and suddenly I could hear the muffled voices deep in their rubber throats trying to get out. Paul's hours of work were instantly drawn into focus for me. These puppets were not facsimiles of life; they were actors waiting for their voices, for their moves, and like the rest of us a chance at that little slip between two eternities that we call life. From my perspective as a writer, this moment was the single most important thing that happened in the studio that morning. I would devote a few sentences to the facts concerning the painting of the faces, but the real mystery that I would focus on would be the sneeze. What happens when a two hundred fifty pound puppeteer sneezes in his studio? That was where the tension was, the life-and-death drama, the mystery of a seemingly ordinary morning." (*The Horn Book*, September–October 1985, p. 530)

Jacqueline Jackson

In an interview, Jacqueline Jackson said, "When you're fishing, you don't stop to clean a fish as soon as you catch it. You keep throwing in your line as fast as you can while the fish are biting. If you come to a hard spot you can't figure out, but the idea's still there ahead of you, solid ground beyond the pig wallow, leap and go on. When all the creative energy's used up you can go back and rewrite and polish to your heart's content, fill in the gaps, clean the fish."

Maurice Sendak

Maurice Sendak has said that his most famous book of all, *Where the Wild Things Are*, is very much rooted in his childhood experience. Every Sunday his relatives would come over, and because Maurice's mother needed to spend some time cooking in the kitchen, she would tell her son, "Maurice, go talk to the relatives."

Sendak said he can remember those relatives, looking down at him with their big huge faces and holding his cheeks in their hands, saying "Oh, you are so cute, I could eat you up." Sendak was a small, sickly child and he says now, "I always had the feeling that if dinner didn't come soon, they might do just that."

Madeleine L'Engle

When Madeleine L'Engle was talking about her book *A Wrinkle in Time*, some students asked her, "How did you get the characters?" Ms. L'Engle replied, "I was an only child, so I gave Meg three brothers because I always wanted brothers. . . . You can give yourself things in books!"

Cynthia Rylant

Cynthia Rylant's anthology of poems *Waiting to Waltz* and her picture book *When I Was Young in the Mountains* both consist of a collage of scenes and moments from Rylant's childhood in Appalachia. The picture book tells of her earliest years, when she lived in the mountains; the anthology of poems focuses more on her early adolescent years in the small Appalachian town of Beaver. Significantly, the first ends with the idea that she never wanted to go anywhere else in the world than her mountain home; the second ends with her longing to see the rest of the world.

L

Building Files of Author Stories

This bibliographical list may be used with the activity "Develop a File of Author Anecdotes" in the "Stories of Authors' Lives" section of chapter 8.

The following texts are a rich source of author anecdotes. Teachers can be invited to search through these articles and others like them for stories about their students' favorite authors. The instructor might provide time for teachers to think through how they might use the stories, or the instructor might simply ask each teacher to find one special story and then tell it to the entire group. The power of a story has a great deal to do with a teacher's ability to tell it well.

Cech, John. "Maurice Sendak: Off the Page." *The Horn Book*, May–June 1986: 503–13.

Cullinan, Bernice. *Literature and the Child*. San Diego, CA: Harcourt Brace Jovanovich, 1981.

Lanes, Selma G. "Ezra Jack Keats: In Memoriam." *The Horn Book*, September–October 1984: 551–58.

Lasky, Kathryn. "Reflections on Non-Fiction." *The Horn Book*, September–October 1985: 527–32.

McKee, Barbara. "Van Allsburg: From a Different Perspective." *The Horn Book*, September–October 1986: 566–71.

Neumeyer, Peter. "The Creation of E. B. White's 'The Trumpet of the Swan': The Manuscripts." *The Horn Book*, January–February 1985: 17–28.

Rylant, Cynthia. "Thank You, Miss Evans." *Language Arts* 62 (September 1985): 460–61.

Silvey, Anita. "An Interview with Robert Cormier, Part I." *The Horn Book*, March–April 1985: 145–55.

———. "An Interview with Robert Cormier, Part II." *The Horn Book*, May–June 1985: 289–96.

Wernick, Robert. "A Lovable Elephant That Youngsters Never Ever Forget." *Smithsonian*, July 1984: 90–96.

Wood, Don; and Wood, Audrey. "The Artist at Work: Where Ideas Come From." *The Horn Book*, September–October 1986: 556–66.

Authors' Anecdotes That Could Inspire New Classroom Rituals, Tools, or Traditions

This set of anecdotes may be used with the activity "Use Author Anecdotes to Introduce New Tools and Rituals" in the "Stories of Authors' Lives" section of chapter 8.

Teachers can discuss ways these author anecdotes might inspire new rituals, tools, or traditions in the classroom. (Some ideas are provided for each one in Workshop Materials N.)

1   Patricia MacLachlan has said that when she reads E. B. White's essays, they make her breathless. Sometimes the essays say something that she has to write down right away in order to keep the words, to save them and be able to think about them later.

2   Cynthia Rylant says, "I protect the books I love best like a mother lioness. I have a copy of a book by James Agee. It's called *Let Us Now Praise Famous Men*. It and his other book, *A Death in the Family*, are most responsible, I think, for my writing. How I write, what I write about. And often I keep one of those books by my bed. . . . When I can't write and think I won't ever again, I reach for Agee. . . ."

3   Melville imagined himself writing for Hawthorne. Allen Ginsberg imagines himself writing for Jack Kerouac. He says, "He's my listening angel."

4   Jean Little, the blind Canadian author, said that her editor began reading edited manuscripts aloud to her. This was so effective that the editor

now reads edited manuscripts aloud to all her authors, even the sighted ones.

5   In order to write *The Trumpet of the Swan*, E. B. White did voluminous research. He kept a folder titled "Source Materials and Letters," filled with sheets with details about birds, and with notes, queries, and clippings on trumpet music. He collected photographs, maps, and song sheets.

Discussion of Authors' Anecdotes That Could Inspire New Classroom Rituals, Tools, or Traditions

These numbered comments relate to the author anecdotes in Workshop Materials M.

1 Students might keep literary scrapbooks in which they would copy or tape passages from the texts that leave them breathless. So often students come across passages they love. These scrapbooks would provide them with a way of retrieving these favorite passages.

2 Students might be asked to keep a stack of their favorite books near them as they write. Students could also meet in small response groups occasionally to tell others what they learn from these favorite books.

3 Perhaps some students need their own "listening angels," authors they aim to please as they write. Students might become more critical readers if they imagined authors like Maurice Sendak or James Howe looking over their shoulders as they reread their work.

4 A new editing ritual might require students to read their final drafts aloud to a friend, listening for the rhythm and precision of the language.

5 When students begin a new piece of fiction they might be given large manila folders in which they, too, could store all the clippings, photographs, and correspondence that they will be collecting. Just as White sent out queries to musicians and zookeepers, students might put a box in a prominent place in the school building titled "Authors' Queries, Information Wanted!"

O

Situations That Can Lead to Mini-Lessons Using Literature

These ideas may be used with the activity "Dramatize the Need to Take Cues from Students" in the "Using Literature as a Resource for Learning About Good Writing" section of chapter 8.

   In small or large groups, teachers can discuss ways they might refer to literature in mini-lessons. Because mini-lessons should be designed in response to students' writing, several possible descriptions of student writing have been included here. For each one, there are many different ways of responding with mini-lessons based on literature. Some of these are presented in Workshop Materials P.

1   Your students' language tends to lack freshness. The words they choose are predictable and clichéd. They need to know that, rather than using the first words that come to mind, writers try to select exactly the right words. Writers do not aim to use big words but instead, to be honest and precise. This leads them to use familiar words in new and surprising ways.

2   Your students don't usually take time to develop their characters, and if they do, they tend to tell the characters' age, height, and hair color. You want your students to appreciate that there are many ways in which writers develop their characters; they present visual descriptions, they show characters in action, and they include characters' dialogue. Always they try to convey a great deal by carefully selecting the most telling details about a character.

3   Your students' writing folders are filled with pieces that summarize the proceedings in the big events of life: birthdays, holidays, trips. You would like students to know that good topics can also involve everyday moments and the little things in life that are important.

4 Some of your students' writing is ornate, laced with flowery adjectives and adverbs. You want them to appreciate the power of simple language and, especially, of precise verbs and nouns.

P

Discussion of Situations That Can Lead to Mini-Lessons Using Literature

The following numbered comments relate to the situations presented in Workshop Materials O.

1   As course instructor, you might want to suggest that poetry is a perfect place to help students begin thinking about word choice. Poets often use old words in the freshest, most surprising ways. Carl Sandburg's fog comes on "little cat feet." Langston Hughes says the bridges in San Francisco are "spun across the water like cobwebs in the sky." Myra Cohn Livingston describes waves at the beach by saying, "When you squint, you can see hundreds of yellow sunshine spitballs."

2   Teachers might be tempted to present all they know about character development in one mini-lesson. Instructors might want to remind them that they cannot squeeze six points into a two-minute meeting preceding the writing workshop. They can, of course, design a week-long course of study on a topic such as character development, or they can be content to share one tip at a time.

3   It will probably be easy for teachers to find excerpts from fictional writing that illustrate the way authors weave true bits of information into their stories. In addition, teachers might make good use of an article such as Peter Neumeyer's "The Creation of E. B. White's *The Trumpet of the Swan*" in the Jan./Feb. 1985 issue of *The Horn Book*, pp. 17–34. The article details White's research techniques, which include interviews, observation, notes, queries, clippings, and photographs. In some up-per-elementary and secondary level classrooms, students are reading articles like this one.

4 Teachers could select literature samples showing the importance of strong verbs and nouns. They could also read William Zinsser's *On Writing Well* (New York: Harper & Row, 1985), chapters 2, 3, and 13.

Bibliography

Arkin, Alan. *The Lemming Condition.* New York: Harper & Row, 1977.

Atwell, Nancie. *In the Middle.* Upper Montclair, NJ: Boynton/Cook Publishers, 1987.

Barth, Roland. *Run School Run.* Cambridge, MA: Harvard University Press, 1980.

Bissex, Glenda. *GNYS AT WORK: A Child Learns to Write and Read.* Cambridge, MA: Harvard University Press, 1980.

Boomer, Garth. *Fair Dinkum Teaching and Learning.* Upper Montclair, NJ: Boynton/Cook Publishers, 1985.

Calkins, Lucy McCormick. *The Art of Teaching Writing.* Portsmouth, NH: Heinemann, 1986.

———. *Lessons from a Child: On the Teaching and Learning of Writing.* Portsmouth, NH: Heinemann, 1983.

Cech, John. "Maurice Sendak: Off the Page." *The Horn Book,* May–June 1986: 305–13.

Cullinan, Bernice. *Literature and the Child.* San Diego, CA: Harcourt Brace Jovanovich, 1981.

Giacobbe, Mary Ellen. "A Writer Reads, A Reader Writes." In *Understanding Writing: Ways of Observing, Learning & Teaching,* edited by Thomas Newkirk and Nancie Atwell, pp. 114–25. Portsmouth, NH: Heinemann, 1986.(Originally published in 1982 by The Northeast Regional Exchange, Chelmsford, MA.)

Goswami, Dixie; and Butler, Maureen, eds. *The Web of Meaning: Essays on Writing, Teaching, Learning, and Thinking.* Upper Montclair, NJ: Boynton/Cook Publishers, 1983.

Graves, Donald H. *Writing: Teachers & Children at Work.* Portsmouth, NH: Heinemann, 1983.

Hansen, Jane; Newkirk, Thomas; and Graves, Donald, eds. *Breaking Ground: Teachers Relate Reading and Writing in the Elementary School.* Portsmouth, NH: Heinemann, 1985.

Harste, Jerome; Woodward, Virginia A.; and Burke, Carolyn L. *Language Stories and Literacy Lessons.* Portsmouth, NH: Heinemann, 1984.

Holdaway, Don. *The Foundations of Literacy*. Sydney, Australia: Ashton Scholastic, 1979. Distributed by Heinemann, Portsmouth, NH.

Kamler, Barbara. "One Child, One Teacher, One Classroom: The Story of One Piece of Writing." *Language Arts* 57 (September 1980): 680–93.

Lanes, Selma G. "Ezra Jack Keats: In Memoriam." *The Horn Book*, September–October 1984: 551–58.

Lasky, Kathryn. *Puppeteer*. New York: Macmillan, 1985.

———. *Sugaring Time*. New York: Macmillan, 1983.

———. "Reflections on Non-Fiction." *The Horn Book*, September–October 1985: 527–32.

Lortie, Dan. *Schoolteacher: A Sociological Study*. Chicago: University of Chicago Press, 1977.

McKee, Barbara. "Van Allsburg: From a Different Perspective." *The Horn Book*, September–October 1986: 566–71.

Murray, Donald M. *Learning by Teaching: Selected Articles on Writing and Teaching*. Upper Montclair, NJ: Boynton/Cook Publishers, 1982.

———. *Write to Learn*. New York: Holt, Rinehart & Winston, 1984.

Neumeyer, Peter. "The Creation of E. B. White's *The Trumpet of the Swan*: The Manuscripts." *The Horn Book*, January–February 1985: 17–28.

Newkirk, Thomas. "Archimedes' Dream." *Language Arts* 61 (April 1984): 341–50.

Newkirk, Thomas; and Atwell, Nancie. "The Competence of Young Writers." In *Perspectives on Research and Scholarship in Composition*, pp. 185–202. New York: The Modern Language Association of America, 1985.

Rylant, Cynthia. "Thank You, Miss Evans." *Language Arts* 62 (September 1985): 460–61.

———. *When I Was Young in the Mountains*. New York: Dutton, 1982.

Sarason, Seymour. *The Creation of Settings and the Future Societies*. San Francisco: Jossey-Bass, 1972.

———. *The Culture of the School and the Problem of Change*. 2nd ed. Newton, MA: Allyn & Bacon, 1982.

Shaughnessey, Mina. *Errors and Expectations*. New York: Oxford University Press, 1977.

Silvey, Anita. "An Interview with Robert Cormier, Part I." *The Horn Book*, March–April 1985: 145–55.

———. "An Interview with Robert Cormier, Part II." *The Horn Book*, May–June 1985: 289–96.

Smith, Frank. *Insult to Intelligence*. New York: Arbor House Publishing Co., 1986.

———. "Reading Like a Writer." *Language Arts* 60 (May 1983): 558–67.

———. *Reading Without Nonsense*. 2nd ed. New York: Teachers College Press, 1985.

Sowers, Susan. "Reflect, Expand, Select: Three Responses in the Writing

Conference." In *Understanding Writing: Ways of Observing, Learning &
Teaching*, edited by Thomas Newkirk and Nancie Atwell, pp. 76–90.
Portsmouth, NH: Heinemann, 1986, (Originally published in 1982 by
The Northeast Regional Exchange, Chelmsford, MA.)

———. "Six Questions Teachers Ask About Invented Spelling." In *Understanding Writing: Ways of Observing, Learning & Teaching*, edited by Thomas
Newkirk and Nancie Atwell, pp. 47–56. Portsmouth, NH: Heinemann,
1986. (Originally published in 1982 by The Northeast Regional Exchange,
Chelmsford, MA.)

Spencer, Margaret. "Children's Literature: Mainstream Text or Optional
Extra?" In *English in the Eighties*, edited by Robert Eagleson, pp. 114–27.
Sydney, Australia: Australian Association for the Teaching of English,
1982. Distributed by Boynton/Cook Publishers, Upper Montclair, NJ.

Steiner, Vera-John. *Notebooks of the Mind*. Albuquerque, NM: University of
New Mexico Press, 1985.

Trelease, Jim. *The Read-Aloud Handbook*. New York: Viking Penguin Inc.,
1979.

Wernick, Robert. "A Lovable Elephant that Youngsters Never Forget."
Smithsonian, July 1984: 90–96.

White, E. B. *Charlotte's Web*. New York: Harper & Row, 1952.

Wood, Don; and Wood, Audrey. "The Artist at Work: Where Ideas Come
From." *The Horn Book*, September–October 1986: 556–66.

———. *The Napping House*. San Diego, CA: Harcourt Brace Jovanovich,
1984.

Zinsser, William. *On Writing Well: An Informal Guide to Writing Nonfiction*.
Rev. ed. New York: Harper & Row, 1985.